CW01498651

SIM SIM

GEET
CHATURVEDI

Translated from the Hindi by
ANITA GOPALAN
Winner *of* PEN America's
PEN/Heim Translation Fund Grant

PENGUIN BOOKS
An imprint of Penguin Random House

PENGUIN BOOKS

USA | Canada | UK | Ireland | Australia
New Zealand | India | South Africa | China

Penguin Books is part of the Penguin Random House group of companies
whose addresses can be found at global.penguinrandomhouse.com

Published by Penguin Random House India Pvt. Ltd
4th Floor, Capital Tower 1, MG Road,
Gurugram 122 002, Haryana, India

Penguin
Random House
India

First published in English in Penguin Books by Penguin Random House India 2023

Copyright © Geet Chaturvedi 2023
Translation Copyright © Anita Gopalan 2023

ISBN 9780670097289

Typeset in Bembo Std by Manipal Technologies Limited, Manipal
Printed at Thomson Press India Ltd, New Delhi

www.penguin.co.in

To my grandmother, whose palms smelled sweet with guava,
and who remembered her Larkana until her last breath.
—Geet

To my mother Tara, present as a gentle light in my life.
—Anita

CONTENTS

1. My Name is 'I'   1

2. The Old Man's Story   7

3. My Name is 'I'   16

4. The Old Man's Story   27

5. Dil Khush   50

6. My Name is 'I'   53

7. The Old Woman is Silent   61

8. The Book Cover Tells a Tale   72

9. Dil Khush   78

10. My Name is 'I'   83

11. The Old Man's Story   91

12. My Name is 'I'   99

13. The Book Cover Tells a Tale   105

14. Dil Khush   110

15. My Name is 'I'   114

16. The Old Man's Story   120

17. My Name is 'I'   135

18. The Old Woman is Silent   145

19. Dil Khush   152

20. My Name is 'I'   157

21. The Old Man's Story   162

22. The Old Man's Story   187

23. My Name is 'I'   194

24. Dil Khush   198

25. My Name is 'I'   204

26. The Book Cover Tells a Tale   212

27. My Name is 'I'   220

Translator's Note   225

List of Quotations   229

Author's Acknowledgements   233

Translator's Acknowledgements   235

Common Acknowledgements   237

1

MY NAME IS 'I'

'In the beginning there was a river. The river became a road and the road branched out to the whole world. And because the road was once a river it was always hungry.'

—Ben Okri, *The Famished Road*

When I was small, my father sold me like a pumpkin. He would put me on his shoulders and go from room to room, crying out like a street hawker, 'Pumpkin! Fresh juicy pumpkin! Two rupees a kilo! Only two rupees!' I greatly relished this play. My father's shoulder was my favourite picnic spot.

His voice boomed, profound and effortless, in the house, and as soon as it fell on my ears, I squealed with delirious joy, and my feet reflexively thumped towards him to somehow get onto his mighty shoulders.

When I was around six, I don't know what came over me one day that I told him, 'Don't say pumpkin, Pau, say gold—Gold! Fresh shiny gold! Two rupees a kilo!'

Pau burst out laughing, 'So cheap you'll sell gold?'

'That I don't know. But I am gold, not pumpkin,' I said resolutely.

My Pau did not agree. He kept selling me like a pumpkin, whereas I wanted to be sold like gold. The truth is, I was neither gold nor pumpkin, but then don't desires clash in life more than swords? This marked the dawn of a history of a difficult relationship between my father and me, after which I formally dethroned myself, no longer eager to belong among the lofty mountains of his shoulders. Yet, the dream stayed in a mazed corner of my mind, seeking acceptance of my worth.

And the bond remained between his voice and my feet—whenever his voice boomed, my feet still moved but now towards the door. So long as that powerful voice resided in the house, there remained no space for my feet. I walked outside then for a long time in the supposed spatial infinity of the streets: one street in particular.

From Nehru Chowk to Flowers Lane. I have paced this street more than any other by now. And I do not even live at Nehru Chowk, nor have I ever had any reason to go to Flowers Lane. And in the world that walks between the two, I can view every colour of the larger world. In this way, I fancy, my walking is meshed inside the world's walking.

But why do I walk so much? An interesting answer comes from my mother.

One day she said, 'You know, it is Lord Shiva who makes you walk so much.'

I laughed out loud, 'Shiva? Why he?' And my mother told me one of her funny, sad, innocent 'me-in-her-womb' stories:

'This happened before you were born, or rather when I was carrying you. I was always tired from doing all the cooking and housework. One night, out of sheer exhaustion, I slept without doing the dishes. This had never happened before. I hated to leave a pile of unwashed dishes in the kitchen. I was so apologetic about it that I dreamed of those dirty utensils. They emerged from the sink and slimed down the kitchen floor on their dirty bottoms. Like bugs and insects, their number increased rapidly. I got scared. I began reciting the Shiva mantra: *Om Namah Shivay. Om Namah Shivay.* And then a miracle happened! Lord Shiva himself appeared before me. He began dancing in the kitchen, that too on one leg, beating his little drum and wearing an expression of anger on his face. He looked at me with his exquisite red eyes and said, "There is a lot of dirt in your kitchen, child. I can't stay here. Either the dirt stays or I!"

I trembled with fear. Folding my hands together, I said, "I dropped asleep, Bhagwan. But you are all-knowing! Tell me, have I ever left dirty dishes in my kitchen before?"

To this, Lord Shiva said, "Look, child! You eat in clean utensils. And dirty utensils eat into you."

"What should I do, Bhagwan? I am so tired, because of this!" I said, pointing to my swollen belly.

"This?" Lord Shiva looked and smiled, "This is life. It will go on. Keep going on. But child, this filth can't stay. It has to go."

Right after that, all the utensils started marching like an army of ants. I tried to stop them, but no, they kept going. I unwillingly started following them. For long those utensils kept walking, I walked behind them, and you, a part of me, walked along. Suddenly all the dirty utensils disappeared, and my sleep broke.

It was two o'clock in the night when, shaking off my exhaustion, I went to the kitchen and, washing all the dirt, lightened the weight on my soul.

Then, for the first time, I felt you move inside me. Your tiny legs kicked like crazy; it was as though you were marching all over inside my belly. I tried waking your father, but he was fast asleep. That night, you mistook my belly for a playground and drubbed around, battering me from the inside.

I wondered, just a thought, would my child have some sort of affinity for walking? Then, when I saw you were born with a black mole under your right foot, I became certain. In fact, one of my earlier hopes was that you become a sprinter on growing up.' The thought brought a smile to her lips.

'So, this entire play is Shiva's?' I said, teasing her.

'Yes, exactly. And your mole's,' she said with sublime conviction in her own innocence.

'Arré Ma, this is no connection!' I said in amused disbelief.

'Whatever it is, but you do walk all the time,' she said sweetly.

I said in a voice of reproach, 'When you had a direct meeting with Shiva, you should have asked for a motorcar! Now because of your one fault, I have to walk on foot.'

'Not my fault that I fell asleep and didn't wash.' And she made such a face that even an angry Shiva, had he seen her innocence at the time, would have ho ho-ed his loud laughter.

Whenever I remember this tale of my mother, I feel I'd been walking even before I was born! I can feel an ancient fatigue crawling on my feet all the time. Despite that, the days I feel life has come to a full stop, I walk, which reassures me that my life is still moving.

And, of course, there's my 'Imbelo' who walks with me. My sweetheart, Imbelo! My imaginary beloved like Beethoven's 'Immortal Beloved'.

Although she lives in my mind, I need her quasi-existence to ensure my continued existence. I seek to assuage my loneliness by her company. She talks to me about things I want to hear. Her unknowing presence comforts me and gives me self-confidence. Thus, with her at the rendezvous chatting, whispering, throbbing inside me, I find relief.

Together we walk. The surroundings change, but the street never does. I ask her, 'All rivers drop into the ocean one day, but has anyone seen where the street goes and drops off?'

And she says with playful promptness, 'If all the world's streets were gathered together, they would make a nice bun of hair. So, every street walks from its place to tie at my nape.'

I run my hand through her hair and exclaim: 'Look, how many streets are caught in my fingers!'

Looking at all the streets caught in my fingers, she chirps: 'I can see a long journey written on your hand.'

I do wish, sometimes, that she would shut up, but she loves talking. She says staying in your head makes everything interesting. Then all of a sudden, she disappears, chirping, laughing, flipping back her serpentine hair, taking along all of the world's streets that got tacked on to my fingers.

I look at my fingers, the cigarette stuck in them. I won't light it right away. Like an old man, I will dodder along the street and later, seated on a slab of rock in front of Central Hospital, I will gaze a long time at the cigarette before asking a passer-by for a match, and after being refused two, three times, a fourth fellow will pass me a match and then I will light it. Like a long take in a black-and-white film.

And this entire sequence will stretch out in such slow motion that I will begin to see myself as a street. An endless monotonous street that walks so sluggishly it appears stationary. When a river becomes a road, it first loses its current. Then its waters. Then it loses itself.

To become a road is the biggest cruelty that can befall a river.

2

THE OLD MAN'S STORY

'Human memory is a wonderful but fallible instrument . . . The memories residing within us are not engraved in stone. Not only do they tend to fade over the years, they often change or even grow to incorporate extraneous features.'

—Primo Levi, *The Drowned and the Saved*

He has to work so hard to open the thermos, as if the thermos was his whole life, or the girl who had come into his life years ago, whose face he cannot recollect, but the street where she had lived is still vivid in his mind. And he definitely remembers that he had loved her, but how much—that is now a distant, forgotten memory.

It may have been more than sixty years since he first touched her, on the nape of her neck. It had been his first touch of any young woman, and he can recall that his hand had shaken quite violently. He would move his fingers on her nape and the front of her neck, then get nervous, then caress again, then his hand would begin sliding down her front that he would, on getting nervous, pull back again. The amused girl had burst out laughing, watching his trembling hands. And that had shaken him even further.

His hand frequently slides in an attempt to open the thermos. At every pressure of his hand, the thermos simply makes a hissing sound. Each time he lets go, wipes his hand on the napkin spread on his lap, then the neck of the thermos, and begins anew, the persuasive pressure on the neck.

Half a century later, that girl is laughing again. The sound of her voice is coming from inside the thermos.

Basar Mal Jetharam Purswani reminds himself that he is now old and grey, having lived so long, and he shouldn't remember anything he ever felt, but his self is constantly nudging memory to remember the girl whom he had kissed when he was around sixteen, sitting under the lone shady tree, growing in the compound of a desolate madrasa in the town of Larkana, in Sindh province of Pakistan, while she was narrating to him the Sufi poet Shah Abdul Latif's ballad 'Sassi-Punnu'.

In the story that she narrated, Sassi, the beautiful daughter of a washerman and Punnu, the prince of the land, fell madly in love and married despite fierce family opposition. The prince's brothers so detested the marriage that they got the prince drunk on the night of the wedding and took him away to some unknown land. When day broke, and Sassi found her husband missing, she went berserk, searching, scouring every piece of ground. The merciless hot deserts of the Thar blistered her unshod feet and parched her lips. But she, unaware in the anguish that had seized her body completely, galloped barefoot on the burning hot sand. The bright emptiness of the desert, the dazed emptiness of the heart. Two camel riders tried to take advantage of her astounding beauty. She cried out imploringly to Mother Earth to take her in. The earth parted, and Sassi sank deep into its darkness. Only her veil stood on the surface, part sunk in the ground, part swaying in air. Its shadow wavering on the hot sand.

Sitting next to him in the desolate madrasa, his girl, the narrator, became Sassi. She felt the soles of her feet welt. She looked at them and wondered how many steps she could now walk. The hot arid breeze parched her nostrils and her lips. She could almost smell the hot desert wind, and the anguish seeping through time. Smoothening her veil, she stared at the madrasa's tall wall for a while and said, 'Love is a half-sunk swaying veil, part of it always remaining invisible to the eye. And so we imagine the part we see as the whole.'

She paused for breath, 'You know, all stories are incomplete.'

Basar Mal puts pressure on the thermos yet another time. This time, the lid yields and hisses open. He is unable to stop its impetus, and a little milk spurts on the newspaper lying on the table. He gets some old paper from the dustbin and dabs the newspaper, then pours some milk into the cup-shaped cap of the thermos.

It is getting dark outside. In some time, the electricity will also be gone. Before that, he has to finish reading all three evening papers, file important news cuttings, clean the mould that may have found a breeding ground on the books of the back racks, and on the way back home, he also has to get some medicines for Mangan's Ma. He wonders if he could ever see himself as 'whole', like the veil above ground? Rolling up the sleeves of his white kurta, which looks more like a shirt, he sprinkles some coffee powder into the milk and goes to the window.

Bringing the mug close to his lips, he feels the deep aroma of coffee and the rising steam. He tries to remember the girl's aroma, and again in the region between his upper lip and nose, there rises the warmth of that girl's breath, like the steam of the coffee.

Perhaps the girl's lips were brown in colour. Definitely not pink. No. And her skin was like coffee mixed in milk.

The street can clearly be seen from the library window. On the other side of the road is a motley collection of buildings. Opposite the library, four feet to the left, is another window with yellow shutters and a lattice of big yellow flowers, above which a parapet juts out, perhaps of tin, whose colour is also yellow. He looks at that window and, taking one more sip of his coffee, remembers the kiss given more than sixty years ago.

Back then, while kissing, his hands had shaken; now, while walking, his legs shake.

An erratic vein within him is rippling with a wave of wonderment, that the girl whose face eludes his memory, and whose name he's uncertain about, only the aftermath of a kiss, the hot quivering lips, the trembling hands and some other similar graphics he can recall, and these descriptions too, before today, had not been in his memory, now they are—and hence we can say that he remembers—but why is he suddenly stricken by her memory? Where was this girl all these years?

Old love is like the veil, part sunk in the ground, part swaying in air. One can neither wrap it around oneself nor carry it along. Its shadow wavers on the sands of time.

Sitting against the madrasa wall, the girl had said one day, 'You know what I saw today? I was putting out the washing on the roof when I looked down and saw a very old couple walking slowly along the street, holding a walking stick in one hand, and each other's hand in the other. Whether the man was supporting the woman, or it was the other way round, I don't know. They were hobbling along, lovingly supporting each other.'

Sixteen-year-old Basar Mal asked impatiently, 'So? What's so special about it?'

The girl said, 'Nothing special, yet that scene got nailed into my memory like a picture. Don't you think they are lucky to be together at such a ripe age?'

Basar Mal laughed it off and said merrily, 'Come to my house, and I will show you all my grandparents, maternal and paternal. See for yourself how old they are. Double old than everyone else's.'

'Double old?' her eyes twinkled with amusement momentarily, then became doleful again, 'But do they hold hands?'

Basar Mal realized that this was not the time for mischief. He replied awkwardly, 'No.'

The girl drew a deep breath and said, 'That's what I want to tell you. When you and I are old, will we be together? Promise me if we are still together, we will walk like that, holding each other's hands.'

Basar Mal held her hand and said with great self-confidence, 'Okay. I promise.'

The girl burst out laughing. Then she proceeded to tease him that she had always known that he was the one for whom she had deigned to come down on this earth.

Basar Mal Jetharam Purswani leans against the library wall, coffee mug in one hand, to examine the other hand: perhaps he had pressed this hand in hers to promise eternal companionship, to hold hands in their old age? Today, he's old, but where's the girl? Suddenly he feels very lonely. After a long time, he is once again acutely aware that he had miserably failed to live up to the most beautiful promise of his life. He closes his eyes and tries to imagine the girl, and suddenly the room smells strongly of the aroma of ripe guava.

There is no one in the room. Yet the feeling of someone's presence is oddly there. Palpable in its absence, giving his loneliness company.

He stares out the window at the vehicles zipping past, but in reality, his eyes are peering into six-decade-old memories. His introversion digs into him, probing, interrogating:

What he's been trying to recall over coffee, did it really happen that same way? All of it? Or, was his memory filling up its gaping blanks after so many years, by fabricating new scenes and stories similar to the ones it had seen several times in films or books of fiction, seemingly similar extraneously, but perhaps, with different sensibility? The feelings resurging after sixty-odd years might've been verily the same even then? Or, the way they were then might've now come back exactly the same?

He does not know where the girl went. He was to take her to Shahdadkot. She pestered him that they should run away to Lahore. But Lahore was far. And so, he had refused and said they would first go to the closer Shahdadkot. Perhaps even then, while refusing, Basar Mal Jetharam Purswani's legs would have shaken. The girl would have shown her displeasure. Then she would have told him not to talk to her anymore, then, pouting, she would have sulked to one side on the steps of the desolate madrasa.

Basar Mal thinks of the pout and the sulk that amused and excited him—on the steps of the madrasa, or the lawns of the old college, or the park, that later was to be called Jinnah Park, and where he saw for the first time a living, breathing man hit by a bullet, fly up three cubits and fall back down dead.

Memory draws a blank after that. They did not make it to Shahdadkot after all. The girl vanished somewhere. It was rumoured that she had been abducted by the Baloch. Then there were whisperings about her running away with the Pashtuns. Then it was heard that she had gone away to Miro Khan. Then it was heard . . . then it was heard . . . and one day, one stopped hearing about her.

Slowly, his memories are coming back and filling his mind. He had never been a victim of amnesia, but he had, for many years, deferred recollecting his past in any systematic way.

Is his life nearing its end? And knowing it, are his memories now rushing to him?

There is nothing more personal than memory. Nothing more manipulated than it. The struggle of memory with memory, struggle of memory with oblivion, struggle of memory with imagination, struggle of memory with truth, and struggle of memory with beliefs and suppositions—at how many levels this goes on, and in how many worlds simultaneously—that someone said, *the human is a memorial to the multiple worlds of the human in oblivion.** Many things would have happened unconsciously, without his knowledge. The imagination would have fed on oblivion to create a memory of its own. And this memory would have then begun to irrigate the barren land of the sovereign region of fiction, relishing its 'found refuge' kind of meaning inside the imagination. And . . .

Brusquely cutting short his thoughts, he whispers: 'Imaginary memories? No, my memories aren't imagined memories. Every sliver is true. My memory is the memory of a refugee who was forced to leave his soil. I am a Sindhi. I live in India. My Sindh is in Pakistan. How many Sindhis are in India? Millions. How much of Sindh is in India? As much as a word in the national anthem. The place not in India is mentioned in the national anthem of India. This is "memory". Memory is my homeland. No one can take it away from me. Those who lose their homeland have memory as their homeland.'

Someone stirs at the yellow window opposite and, drawing the curtain across, covers its face. This is not the kind of kinesics Basar Mal was waiting or hoping for. Still, that small activity at that flower-latticed window disrupts his concentration and gives his internal monologue a break, but not before the voice whispers, 'What are you remembering, Basar Mal? Homeland or love?'

'Both.'

'Why?'

'Because I lost both,' he answers, murmuring softly so as not to hear it himself.

Remembering a kiss of long ago, Basar Mal Jetharam Purswani unconsciously leaves a little coffee in the mug and goes towards the bookracks. He moves his hand over the books. The dust of books clings to his fingers. Hunching up, he looks at the mouldering dust settled on them. With agonizing deliberation, he pulls out the bottom-most book from the rack. It is a timeworn, tattered book. With a rag hanging from the rack, he dusts it. Carefully taps it, flaps it and, for some time, keeps inhaling it. It is the Sindhi poet Shah Abdul Latif's ballad 'Sassi-Punnu'.

Coming to his table, he starts reading in a husky and quavering old voice. His voice is like the veil, part sunk in the ground, part swaying in air. Its shadow wavering on a mirage of hope.

3

MY NAME IS 'I'

'Only from our stories can we discover that our stories have come
to an end, otherwise we would go on living as if there were still
something for us to continue (our stories, for example); that is, we
would go on living in error.'

— Imre Kertész, *Liquidation*

I stood in front of the library, little knowing it would turn
my world upside down. The house-like structure stood,
quiet and forlorn, with its mud-pantiled architecture,
wooden blinds on windows and padlocked door, appearing
corpselike even in broad daylight like some sort of old
bygone government health centre, and giving no indication
from any angle that it could also be a library. The entire
place had an air of derelict sadness. Perhaps that's why,

standing there in front of it, I remembered Pau's face, a face marked by anguish and annoyance.

Perhaps, Pau honestly thought I took pleasure in annoying him. But that was not always the case. On the contrary, I could tell he got upset seeing me happy.

There was his annoyance at hearing music coming from my room. He would immediately drop in, pull out the wire, wrap it around the tape recorder, pick up the recorder, and trot out. All the while, his dagger-sharp eyes would glare 'no more happiness for you, son', which shivered my spine into pieces.

Then there was his continuing displeasure at seeing me sleep into the mornings. He would rudely shake me—I am convinced that it was to interrupt the smile playing on my face—and yell in my ear, 'It's ten o'clock. Get up and study.'

'What should I study?' I would ask sleepily, for I had finished my college exams, the results were also out, and I had passed with good marks.

'Read your course books again. You never know from where they'll ask questions in the job interview. I remember they had asked me a chemistry question out of the blue. If only I'd answered, I would have been someone else and somewhere else today!'

'That was a different era, Pau, this is different. This is 2007. The twenty-first century!' I would try to reason out.

But every time, like a stubborn child, he yelled, 'No. No. No. Times haven't changed. Read.' And I retorted,

'Don't tell me again and again, Pau. That's why I hate reading.'

Such conversations ended the way all our conversations ended these days:

1. Disappointed in me, my Pau would leave the room with bowed head, and withdraw to his room.
2. Disappointed in Pau, I would leave the house in annoyance, and walk out.

With an ocean of regretful anger erupting inside me, I alternately berated myself for having hurt Pau, or cursed Pau for hurting me.

While walking, I narrated to my Imbelo the illogical antics and unreasonable demands of my father, to which she once said, 'Why do you keep condemning your father?' It then occurred to me that perhaps I tend to scorn everything he does, or perhaps even my ordinary remarks are construed as criticism.

With books, I had established a shifting, complex relationship—a relationship filled with less love, and more annoyance.

And I held my father responsible for it.

I remember, in my childhood years, Pau delighted in bringing me children's books every month. I loved the books, a pleasure I indulged in, to the extent that I slept with them beside me in bed. One day, on the way back after buying me a book, Pau and I went to his friend's place. We used to call him Wrestler Uncle. He was a heavily built man with a thick moustache and thicker arms. His son, Ramu, was eight years older than me but treated me his age. He was my hero, my big brother.

The door was open. Ramu was screaming while Uncle smacked him on the face, holding him by the throat. My Pau hastily went to separate them, but Uncle was in a rage. He pushed Pau away and, with agile hands, lifted his son and threw him on the bed the way he would slam an opponent wrestler down in the arena ring. Then he trumpeted like an elephant, 'Beware, if you get up from bed!'

Ramu lay there crying, agonizing, groaning. I was numbed with terror by the whole grotesque scene, not knowing what crime Ramu had committed. Uncle finally, at Pau's insistence, opened his mouth, 'This little rascal, he was reading a novel. You hear me? Such a young fellow and reading a novel!'

'It's not a crime, my friend, that you should beat him so mercilessly,' Pau said softly, in Ramu's defence.

But ignoring my father's soothing tone, Uncle continued angrily, 'I will break his leg if he reads a novel again. He won't read his course books, no sir, as if his grandmother would die if he touched them. But he'll happily read a novel the whole day, that too, hiding under the bed. I'll kill the bastard, make mincemeat out of him.'

My father's eyes flickered briefly with mischief. 'Which novel are you reading, Ramu? Who's your favourite author?'

Ramu merely groaned in pain. He didn't have the courage to answer. His father didn't give him a chance to answer. Pat came the reply, 'Maharaj, what will he tell?

Okay, he was reading a novel, but a Hindi novel! See? Has anyone in this country prospered by reading Hindi? Ask me, how I struggle every day so that he studies in an English medium school. My life has been sucked out paying his fees, still, somehow I'm managing. See? And this sahib, he leaves his course textbooks and reads a Hindi novel! O foolish child, if you want to read anything, read in English. At least your English will improve. But no, you'll read in Hindi. Goddamn Hindi!'

My father tried to pacify him, 'Arré, you too grew up doing everything in Hindi, no? Then why are you beating him for it? Hindi is our language.'

Uncle flared up. It was like adding ghee to the fire. Affronted, he crackled, 'What will he do with Hindi? Sell pani puri? Or set up a samosa stall? Or cycle rickshaw? Or pickpocket on the local train?'

And once again he started beating Ramu, now more out of desperation. 'Just why don't you read English ré!'

Wrestler Uncle might have been the only father in the world who beat his son for reading a book written in his mother tongue!

'Pau, let's get back home!' I whispered in my father's ears, agitatedly, wanting to flee the scene.

Only after returning home, it dawned upon Pau that he had put me in a government Hindi medium school. And so, I read all books in Hindi, talked in Hindi, listened to Hindi songs, and watched Hindi films. Nothing in my life needed English. All my work got done in Hindi. English, as a subject in school, was taught through Hindi, like Hindi. I still remember how my English teacher would teach us verb forms, making us say 'Buy-Bogut-Bogut' for 'Buy-Bought-Bought'. It was the principal who, overhearing it one day while taking rounds, had corrected us.

My father mused upon his failures—blaming them all on his not knowing English. According to him, there were two types of people in India:

1. Successful people, who knew English, who were powerful everywhere—from the street to the Parliament, and ordered others around.
2. Failed people, who did not know English, spoke Hindi or vernacular, and obeyed orders.

Only politics was such that one could govern without knowing English, but to be successful in it required money-power and muscle-power, which we particularly lacked. That's why my father never considered this third option.

The demonic act of Wrestler Uncle had a great effect on my father. His behaviour changed. Now, he forbade me from reading Hindi books. He brought the English versions of Hindi comics and magazines instead. But I found no joy in reading them in English. I had to look every word up in the dictionary. It was so tiring! After slogging it out for a few days, I accepted defeat and went back to Hindi books, displeasing my father greatly. One day, I found that my Hindi storybooks were all gone. They had been neatly replaced with English books and magazines.

Ironically, I couldn't tell Pau that I didn't understand a word in them. I just pretended to read, and his eyes would light up watching me read. He would say, 'Read it out loud.' And I would read them out aloud. I would read something else for something, which would mean something else, and my father would be so filled with pride watching me read English that I could never tell him I was reading it all wrong—because I didn't know to read right. He didn't either. Perhaps that's why his happiness never broke. To tell the truth, he doesn't doubt my English even today.

But all this made me uneasy. Where I would earlier drown myself in books, my mind now repulsed the very sight of them. The letters of the English alphabet went in circles before my eyes like a roundabout, making me giddy. I panicked. The result: it butchered my passion for reading. I felt a growing irritation in me for books.

English had earned my bitter hatred. That language made me acutely aware of my failures. Hindi did the same thing to me, and I began to hate it about as much as English. I daydreamed that I was an expert in German, French, Spanish or Chinese, that I no longer needed English or Hindi, and then hated myself for seeing such stupid dreams.

But I could never be vocal about my hate. Although my father still made me learn my lessons in Hindi, he was 'obsessed' with English. Whenever he sensed that I was avoiding English, he would shut himself in his room, deeply hurt, and forgo food and water.

This was the wonder drug he chose for showing his displeasure and anger towards us.

It was a ruse we fell for all the time. We asked to be forgiven and cajoled him into opening the door. My weeping mother always feared that he would do something untoward, and I would be responsible for that. Somehow, his antics triggered a similar worry in me, which remained through the years, driving me to hide all my desires, my likes and dislikes, and my fears from him. Whenever arguments went out of control, I wore my slippers and walked out of the house.

This street was my refuge.

This library was going to be my second refuge.

But how did I get here?

For this, I will have to lay out the details of the place and every moment of that evening:

If you did not know that place, it was quite possible that you'd pass through the same street year after year, yet never sight it. From Nehru Chowk to Farver Line ('Flowers Lane' actually—but it had been broken apart and made into Farver Line, and if you ever took the real name, it would only fetch ignorance and confusion). Coming from Nehru Chowk, that smallish library was on the right side with a board announcing its name in Arabic Sindhi. The name had also been there in Hindi and English, but those were just a blur now. An electric wire still hung from the top with an empty bulb holder, an indication that a bulb illuminated the board once. There was a vast compound encircling it, with a jumble of trees and overgrowth.

I, who used to pace this street twenty times in a day, noticed this place called Sindhu Library for the first time when I was walking down the street immediately after a notorious Mumbai rain—capable of giving any nose a cold and any road a slush—wearing flip flops.

Now, flip flops squelch, splash mud, and after a good rain it is risky to wear them, for they can splatter muck any time on you or others. The bottom of my white jeans—I had ripped open the hem to cleave the threads so that their crisp lengths dangled down and those now were being mushed—was covered with mud, and the splotches had reached up to my back pockets. But at the time, I was very unaware of the antics of the wet slush.

Halting five steps before the library, I had fished out a cigarette from my pocket and, snapping a match, lit it. While throwing the burning matchstick into the puddle to my left, I felt someone's gaze on me that was climbing up from my left ankle. I can never forget the delicious, sharp thrill that had sliced through me. That gaze had fallen on my flip flops first. Then it had paused on my jean-covered ankle. Then I had felt that gaze piercing my shin. Then on the knee, then further up. Bending down I surveyed my jeans, and realized that lumps of slush had latched on to them like leeches.

And instinctively my eyes went towards my left, where a building stood. I was ten steps away from the window of its ground-floor flat. It was a yellow shutter window with yellow flower lattice, and above it, a parapet jutted out made of tin, which was also yellow in colour. In that yellow window, a girl's face and body could be seen to the extent that a window can show. It was the piercing gaze of the girl that was down on my pants, flip flops, and the muck. She, too, would have felt my eyes on her, I suppose, for she lifted her head and looked straight into my eyes.

There was absolutely no expression either on her face or in her eyes. I do not know what was there in her gaze that my shin stung and throbbed. She had wrapped her fingers around the window grille. I cannot recollect what she had worn because I could see only her face, which among the yellow shutters, lattice, and parapet, also looked yellow. Her face was an arid, parched landscape as if someone had sandpapered it. Perhaps she had just woken up. Her hair was scattered in a certain manner, and, if not locks, a few loose strands certainly dangled in front of her face.

But if truth be told, she was simply standing—and any addition to it would merely be a figment of my fecund imagination.

Nonetheless, behind that blank impassivity, I had sensed an expression of bold disdain, because after looking me directly in the eye, ideally, she should have moved away from the window, but instead of moving away, she once again slid her gaze down to fix it back on the muck, guiding my gaze down as well.

It might not have been disdain, I thought, several days later stopping at the same spot, but in her gaze, there definitely was a silence, despair and wait.

The entire time that evening, her gaze wrapped around my shin like an amulet. While returning from Farver Line, I had paused again in that same place. There was no one now at the window. A yellow curtain fluttered. Along with the breeze, it alternately ballooned away to show the milky white of the tube light inside, or clung to the window lattice. During the course of standing in this manner, my gaze had turned to the other side of the road and fallen on Sindhu Library right opposite the window.

I previously mentioned it was not a place that was spontaneously noticeable. Still, I could sense an abject emptiness surrounding it, even though there wasn't an inch of vacant space on either side of the street. In the large compound, there lay heaps of building material, and the gate wasn't even secured with a lock. The courage to sneak inside to be able to watch that yellow window for some time acquainted me with Sindhu Library.

It was hard to see the pantile-roofed library sequestered behind a screen of piled brick, cement, crushed rock, sand and gravel, long iron rods, and a lot more paraphernalia. When I sneaked in the first time, night had already fallen. Everything was dead and silent, as if the roaring city had suddenly gone still. When I went again the following afternoon, I found a padlock on the door. A house sparrow was busily pecking at it.

Those days, asleep or awake, I was rankled by the memory of that girl—'Who's she? Is she my Imbelo, who has emerged from my mind and taken a shape?'

That girl was a magical mystery I wanted to solve.

4

THE OLD MAN'S STORY

'. . . the memory of a certain image is but regret for a particular moment . . .'

—Marcel Proust, *Swann's Way*

Basar Mal Jetharam Purswani knows he is old and will probably die soon, however, there are some impatient people who want to kill him. But today, he does not want to think about it. He just wants to hear the laughter coming from the thermos. For a while, he sits still, savouring it.

The girl had once brought with her a black-and-white picture to show him. She had worn a loose pleated sharara. Covered her head with a dark-coloured veil. Folded her hands in front. An aroma of guava had wafted from the picture. Whoever comes from Larkana, their palms smell sweet with guava. That day, they were sitting under the guava tree when unthinkingly, Basar Mal Jetharam Purswani started rubbing the guava leaves on her palms. Smearing its sap on his thumb, he applied a *tika* mark on her forehead. And a little above, he put that sap in her parting too. The girl had burst into giggles. Playfully, she had then clapped her palms on Basar Mal's face. And laughing, chirping, she had galloped away. In this excitement, a small drop of the leaf sap fell on the picture. Basar Mal had, sitting under the tree, long wiped the picture with the edge of his pyjamas.

He smiles. Even half a century ago, he had smiled the same way. A lopsided smile, lifting one corner of his mouth.

He pulls out a rag from the drawer and picks up a broom from his side. Getting behind the rack, he starts with his cloth. Slowly. Cautiously. Then with the broom, he starts tapping the books. The damp, musty smell of the mould spreads in the vicinity. With the back of his palm, he rubs the irritation in his nose, then pulls out some books from their places. A book, in its effort to move out, leaves its cover binding behind and emerges bare. He frowns.

'Oh, my sweet child!' he says, pursing his lips in pity. 'Why do you sulk so much?'

He deposits the decrepit book and the cover on the table, then resumes, spreading twenty-five to thirty books out on the floor. Mould had bred on all of them. The pages of some books had turned so yellow and wet that they would come loose with a mere touch. The paper felt like pulp. With the rag, he starts wiping the books that had bindings made of cloth or rexine. Paperback books, he taps gently with his broom.

When the girl cried and wailed, he would, in his youthful exuberance, tap a leafy branch of the guava tree gently on her back. Then plucking a leaf from the branch, he would stick it in her dangling waist-length plait. Then tuck the entire branch into the shoelace that secured the braid end. 'Look, you've grown a tail!' he would say and gush with laughter. Most times, the girl forgot her wailing and joined in his laughter or, feeling embarrassed, raised her hand to hit.

He peers at the roof over the rack. The roof is mud-pantiled, and he is unable to see anything. He climbs up a stool and examines the rack. The top rack is drenched. He pulls out the books. The plywood has bloated and opened up. Some books are still stuck on it. Some have left their marks on it, coming unstuck. He fingers the books. The water had seeped in deep. He again scans the roof. Since when had the water been dripping down? His old eyes had failed to see. His ears had failed to hear the sound of the falling drops. Why hadn't anything within him tugged or warned him?

An old mothball that hadn't yet fully vaporized falls from the top. It had, however, lost its roundness. He starts wiping the rack with the rag. Because of all the dampness, mustiness, and wetness, the rag wouldn't slide any faster.

Once, he had burst a ripe guava on the girl's shoulder. Her shoulder and back peeked out of the wide-necked kameez. He kept the guava on the bare skin and, with his thumb, began pressing it down. The girl squirmed with pain. The guava ripped open from the middle. He took the two halves in his hands and started rubbing one half on her back. The girl groaned again and pinched his nose hard. Giving his head a sharp jerk, Basar Mal freed his nose and began rubbing the other half, too. The girl felled him with a push.

As she was leaving, Basar Mal had taken out his handkerchief from the pyjama pocket and wiped her back. Softly. His hand moved, but his eyes were fixed on the lone mole on her nape. There were scratch marks by its side left by fingernails. His stare lingered on the mole, his mind lingered on the scratches, and his hand wouldn't slide any faster.

* * *

The Larkana of his memory was ruled by the deep scent of guava and the sweet laughter of a girl. Every love is filled with a fragrance. His love was filled with the scent of guava. The scent hung heavily over the gullies, alleyways, markets. Her laughter hung over the landscape of his heart. He would fondly call her Jaam, which meant guava. An eighteen-year-old girl who loved reading books and telling stories, and met him despite restrictions fastened on her outside the door. They used to meet almost every third day secretly at the madrasa. He was a seventeen-year-old lad who, perched on the mud wall of his house, counted cars whizzing past on the highway or scribbled on loose sheets. One day, he limned his love for her, especially things he couldn't say in front of her.

One day, two days, seven days . . . he kept writing for ten whole days.

In the next meeting, he said, 'I have written a hundred-page letter for you.'

She said, 'One hundred pages? What have you written?'

'Here, read it yourself.'

'You're mad. It will take me twenty days to read one hundred pages. And *khuda na khasta*! if I fall asleep while reading it, then?'

'Then what?'

'Then my father and brother will see the letter flopped on my chest, and they will read everything in just two hours. Then they'll give me a good beating for the next two hours. Then you, for the next two days. That's what will happen.'

'You won't be able to hide my letter?'

'I have to work so hard in hiding your love from them, if I have to hide this epic letter too, won't I die? Please don't write me any letter-shetter.'

'And what has already been written, what about that?'

'Bury it. All the pages. The angel of writing will come in my dream for one hundred nights, and every night, read me a page of the letter,' she said and laughingly took his hand.

'I have written them with my heart. My hundred pages of pure love. You really won't read it? Really?'

She relented, laughing, peeping out the window of the madrasa, 'Okay, for now, read me your best page.'

'A short one,' she said, imploringly, teasingly.

Filled with a new enthusiasm, he thumbed through the
pages and satisfied with one, started,

> *I will come to you as a memory.*
> *Like the way a tree, waking on a languid morning,*
> *finds its body wet with dew*
> *and is filled with a memory of rain.*
> *Like the way you awaken one day at first light*
> *and the memory of the night's dream*
> *pulsates on your left breast as bliss.*
> *Like a boat washed up on the shore*
> *stilled by the memory of the ocean's touch.*
> *Like a butterfly lazy on a flower*
> *opening a memory of its favourite colour.*
> *Like a kite on a string*
> *measuring out memory of the sky.*

She laughed, running her hand through her unplaited hair.

> *I will come to you as a dream.*
> *Before falling asleep*
> *when whisperings of the dreams are inaudible,*
> *you'll keep for me a corner in your sleep.*
> *At the third watch of the night,*
> *I'll come in that heedless sleep*
> *as a heedless smile.*
> *I'll come as a nudge on your shoulder*
> *in a crowded street. I'll come*
> *as a romance-packed Friday night.*

I will come to you as wait.
When your feet are tired after standing for centuries,
I will come as the grounded comfort of sitting down.
Someday I will come as a hiccup in your throat.
Someday while gulping water
as a cough rising from your chest.

He went on pompously,

You will look at someone else and remember me.
You will feed someone else
and imagine its taste in my mouth.
At the ring of the doorbell,
you'll welcome someone else, but it is me
you will be waiting for.
Someone else will tickle you,
but you'll beg me to spare you.

I will come in these ways, more ways,
in every form,
and you won't be able to prevent me
from coming to you ever!

He closed it dramatically.

She laughed harder. Perhaps at his swagger. He was suddenly embarrassed. She laughed, their shadows stretched.

The day folded
into the future
taking another name.

The rest of the letter remained unread, unowned, the portent of what his future love letters could become, the relevant information quietly getting encoded in their DNA.

That day, after returning home, he stitched those hundred pages together with a big needle and a thick thread, the way it was taught in the book-binding class in school. Those pages now looked like a rough notebook. He titled it 'Hundred pages of love and one word of refusal'. He hunted for a small wooden box, placed the freshly sewn pages, scattered some guava leaves on top, and nailed the box shut. At night when everybody was asleep, he buried it in the backyard.

He trusted the angel of writing. More than the angel, her words.

That page of love, because it was read out loud, remained etched in his memory.

The country was partitioned. Riots followed. He lost the land along with the buried treasure. And he lost Jaam. At first, he couldn't comprehend why the riots were happening. It was some time before he gradually came to understand that the English had partitioned the country— this side Pakistan, that side Hindustan, which seemed strange to him. If you saw a picture of his teenage years (although he might not have any pictures left), you'd say lo, he's a Muslim youth! There was no significant difference between the two communities in the places where he grew up. Their food habits, language, attire, everything was the same. They relished the Eid seviyan and lighted the Diwali lamps. Of course, they had disagreements and disputes, they would be hurt and wounded, but the cells darned their bodies so strong and complete that the wounds immediately healed, the skin smoothened and looked so young that no one could guess the age of their culture. The same Hindus and Muslims suddenly turned savagely violent. The pitiless English pointed their finger and sowed wounds. Then, they lay their fingers in the healing wound to divide things. The country cracked, then split apart. An ocean welled up. The year was 1947. You might unconsciously think of it as just a page of history; for Basar Mal, it was damnation for life. The politics of power affects them the most who have nothing to do with either politics or power.

Basar Mal somehow managed to cross the border, carrying his Sindh through piles of corpses, tangles of screams and cries. He took the Mirpur Khas route (and not the Lahore one) to reach Kota, then, spending a week in the crowded Kota refugee camp, as one among the mass anonymity, snuck into the batch of Delhi-bound Sindhis— the way a nameless twig joins a stream of water and reaches somewhere, and refuging this way at various camps in different cities eventually reached Mumbai.

He could never learn where Jaam went! A dream, an image kept coming back to him, resplendent in evocation: He is digging the earth. Three people appear from the exhumation, faceless, yet speak their names one after another as if taking a bow—Shah Abdul Latif. Sassi. Punnu.

His soul was a faraway city invisible on maps: a city lit by lanterns of his love.

One day, a wandering dervish prophesied, *Son, what you've lost, you'll find again in books.* That same evening, on an impulse, he bought a second-hand book from a street vendor near Flora Fountain. There was a pressed-up dried rose among its pages. A familiar aroma came from it—he could sense it, feel it. He suddenly became aware that he could discern the sweet scent of guava in a rose.

Slowly, he began to know the other Sindhi refugees who, like him, had come from across the border. These Sindhis didn't have much money. While fleeing to India, their women had, with great effort, hidden inside their wide-bottom pyjamas a nose-ring or two, earrings, finger rings, and other such articles—which became their assets in these trying times. Life's battle, now, was to survive and settle and acculturate. They embroidered women's clothing, sewed buttonholes and hemmed falls on sarees; they stacked butter papdi on their bamboo stand, or rendered their Sindhi flavour to the Mumbai vada pav. From cheap labour to brokerage, from petty thefts to contract killing, they did all kinds of odd jobs.

They lived from day to day in refugee camps, at railway stations and on footpaths. For many years, they relived their past: *Hunger careened like angry spirits. Silent ruins supported nothing. Women corpselike stretched horizontal. Men statued vertical. Roads trespassed into land borders. The weltered tear. Salty blood.* Memories that justified what they felt at present. And somewhere, a name to their heart: *A lost continent,* where the land pulsed with the shock of Partition.

They were perhaps the bitterest years of Basar Mal's life. Those years before getting a decent job and opening a library!

Refugee camps were choked with people and sickness. The Indian government was allotting houses to refugees, but getting one was not easy. Basar Mal was told that in order to get a house it was necessary to have a ration card in his name. And the ration card would be made only when the refugee certificate was shown. And the refugee certificate wouldn't be issued unless he had the papers that proved he had come to Mumbai in India as a refugee from Sindh, Pakistan, at the time of Partition.

He had no paper. No proof.

He told the clerk, 'I speak Sindhi. That's the only proof that I have come from Sindh.'

The clerk replied, 'Anyone can speak a language. Anyone can pretend to be a refugee to get a free house. Bring your papers, and take the house.'

Basar Mal said, 'But I don't have them. I lost my Ammi and Abbu. I lost my family. We had a huge property and a big house in Larkana. I lost everything. The rioters were everywhere, robbing and looting. Would I save my life or gather papers? It's lucky enough that I'm here alive. You tell me, in such circumstances, where do I get the papers from?'

The clerk said crisply, 'You don't have your papers? Come tomorrow!'

And that 'come tomorrow-come tomorrow' extended into days, then weeks. Basar Mal received neither the certificate nor a house. Maybe the babus wanted a bribe. One day, he got into a fight with the officers, and they offered—more as dismissal than anything else—a way out: If five eminent people of Sindhi society give a certificate in writing that they knew Basar Mal and his family in Larkana, then a refugee certificate could be issued to him.

Basar Mal protested, 'But that will take time. Where will I live till then? Diseases have lapped up the camps. They are unfit to live in even for a single day.'

The officer said in a very sweet tone, 'That is your choice, sir! Whether you stay in the camp or on the road. At the bus stop or on the railway platform. You are a refugee. And refugees can live anywhere. I have seen them living inside the big gutter pipes near the Juhu Chowpatty beach. They have happily occupied them. Slowly, they will occupy the whole country.'

Basar Mal became furious, 'We haven't come here to occupy anything. Someone else has taken our land, and we have been forced to come here.'

The sweet tone of the officer was still intact. He said, 'Who has taken it? Jinnah, is it not? So go, go to Jinnah, sir, why have you come here? Go and tell him that you have no place to live. He will grab some more land, create another Pakistan, and give you a place to live.'

Basar Mal's anger rose, 'Why should I go to Jinnah? I am here as an Indian, and will ask for my rights here.'

The officer laughed out loud. He said in his familiar sweet voice, 'But who says you are an Indian? Do you have any document which says you are? Remember one thing, you are not of India, nor of Pakistan. You are a refugee, sir. You think you have spread your wings, but you are very much mistaken!'

'I am a refugee— I have no homeland— I have no claim to my lost past—' Basar Mal had taken years of repeated humiliation to digest this bitter truth. It wasn't something that was his story alone, but of most other refugees like him, who had been uprooted from their land.

He heard similar stories of pain, apathy, suspicion, and humiliation from his fellow refugees, which after a while, he read in newspapers and later in books on Sindhi literature, and, over and over, he concluded that it was only the names of the characters that changed—the fate remained the same.

That was a period when Jinnah's ghost crazily followed him everywhere. When he went to look for a job, the manager sniggered, 'Why are you asking us? Go, ask Jinnah for a job.'

When he thought of continuing his studies, even the intellectual college teachers were sarcastic, 'What will you do with your education? Become another Jinnah, and break this country?'

He said, 'I have no connection whatsoever with Jinnah. I haven't even met him.'

One day, he felt someone was keeping a watch on him. He shared his fear with the elders of the camp. It turned out that the police had cast their suspicion on him. Not just Basar Mal, but from time to time, the police kept every refugee that had come from Sindh under surveillance.

One day, a plainclothesman strolling in an office stopped Basar Mal and asked in typical Marathi style, 'Ae listen! You are a Hindu, no?'

Basar Mal said, 'Yes.'

Policeman: 'Then why do you call your Aai-Baba "Ammi-Abbu"?'

Basar Mal: 'Everyone in our Sindh says it. Hindus, Muslims, everyone.'

Policeman: 'Speak the truth! You are a Pakistani spy, no? And you are hiding here as a Sindhi. It's true, no?'

Basar Mal kept denying it, but the police fellow didn't listen. The result: an order was clamped on him that every evening he had to log his attendance at a nearby police station. Ten days later, thanks to the kindness of a distinguished Sindhi elder, and a bribe, Basar Mal could escape the clutches of that policeman.

That kind elder advised him, 'Son, be careful like a bird.'

For days afterwards Basar Mal watched the birds. He noticed that they were always alert and cautious. Because they were always afraid. A chirping happy bird was, at the core, a frightened bird. The genesis of caution is fear.

Emerging from a world filled with gentle love, he had reached a fearful, coarse world. He was afraid of people. People were afraid of him. For every little thing, he was told to go back to Pakistan. It came sometimes as well-meaning advice, sometimes as a cuss. For every little problem, Basar Mal and the other refugees were held responsible. It was an everyday thing to beat up a Sindhi refugee, on suspicion or without, accusing them of being a Pakistani spy, a member of a child-trafficking gang, or any such pretext.

How many years went by like this! At times, he'd overhear the whispers of his co-workers— 'Sindhi means a Pakistani spy!' 'Trust a snake, but not a Sindhi.'

All this made that sensitive man very sad. But after a time, he stopped listening. He immersed himself in his search, as that kind dervish had suggested, looking for books, looking for people, looking for enchanting moments, looking for Jaam! Meeting people, he began to pick up information— Remember Seth Dayal Das? He lived on Resham Street in Larkana. You know anything about him? Where his family went? He had a daughter, remember?

He had lost his homeland thousands of kilometres away. He sought it in the streets of Mumbai, abiding by his traditions, culture, customs, and language. Angry and alone, he carried his mountain of sorrows and humiliation, not as a sad and despairing man, but as a man singing in his mother tongue songs of his past and his hope.

He had lost his love thousands of kilometres away. He believed love was nirvana. Times when we have lost our love, when God also goes absconding, we must follow the path of books for nirvana. This belief deepened in him with each passing day, each setting moon, and his search broadened.

From the first day itself, he knew that his search would fail. But lord, there is something about a thing called endeavour! Life needs a purpose, no matter how futile.

Time passed by. A procession of many million moments. Basar Mal found a job. Found a place for a library. In a dizzying megalopolis, where the survival instinct overwhelms one and all, who'd give a damn about books? Who'd dedicate a large piece of land to books when land got costlier every year? Mobilize planks for them when wood got costlier every day?

But Basar Mal wanted to imprison the memories of Sindh in his heart. The dervish was right. There was no better medium than language and books. Books started piling steadily, new and second-hand, from bookshops, including the ones lining the footpaths around Flora Fountain. Gradually in Sindhi, Hindi, and English, and sometimes in Marathi, books converged, like people converging from scattered places. A library took shape: Sindhu Library.

Initially, a good many people came to the library. With shovels of memories unrooted from their homeland. To root back by way of books. The library subscribed to many Sindhi newspapers. Every evening, a flock of people gathered there. The old read and reminisced; the young read and questioned—the legacy of Partition thus borne from age to age.

There was always a debate on what had happened in Sindh during the Partition. Almost everyone had the same opinion on the bloodshed in Punjab, but the bloodshed that took place in Sindh was many times propagated as fake news. Acharya Jivatram Bhagwandas Kripalani, a Sindhi, the president of Congress at the time of Partition, and Mahatma Gandhi's confidant, wrote a report soon after the Partition, which is quoted widely in newspapers. In the report, he says:

There was only a slight exodus of the Hindus and Sikhs from Sindh. It did not suffer from any virulent fanaticism.

To whatever faith the Sindhis belonged, they were powerfully influenced by Sufi and Vedantic thoughts. This made for tolerance.

This remark was construed as an insult by those who had lost their people and property in the riots. On the other hand, there were some fortunate ones who, without encountering violence, could cross the border with ease. They largely agreed with the statement. To Basar Mal, this observation was an irresponsible half-truth. He sent his views on the issue to Acharya Kripalani but couldn't know if the letter reached his hands, for he received no reply. Making the contents of the letter as the base, he built his arguments into an article to publish. But finishing it, he felt that it should remain a private text. He still flips the pages of the article, occasionally reading some of it. A part of the article said:

Punjabis fight, they squabble, laugh out loud, cry loud. Hence, their pain is heard. We Sindhis silently bear our pain and get on with our lives, so it is assumed that we don't have any pain. I am not minimizing the sufferings of Punjabis nor diluting their trauma. In fact, they suffered much more than us during the Partition, but our suffering was also immense. We are not merchants of wounds that we compare wounds. We are humans, and we should show compassion.

Who can forget that the fire of communal violence in Sindh that first spread slowly had, by

January 1948, progressed into an inferno of merciless destruction! And then, the remaining Sindhis also packed their belongings. From Sindh, there was not a slight exodus but a considerable one. Today, Sindhis are all across India, scattered in small townships and settlements, simply because it wasn't possible to settle them all together in one place. They were uprooted, taken apart, and dispersed. This became their inescapable fate. Sindh was also a victim of religious fanaticism. In the name of religion, whether there is one murder or one thousand, it is fanaticism and an instance of intolerance.

I had seen Larkana burning and fearing. I had seen a large number of Hindus fleeing the scene to save their lives. Those were the days that put humanity to shame. I do not want to distinguish between the tragedies that befell Sindh and Punjab, nor do I want to see them separately—as the tragedy of Hindus and the tragedy of Muslims. The cataclysm of 1947–48 was a political butchery, whose images are an indelible and essential part of my nightmares.

At the time, a newspaper had run a bold headline: 'The Indian Auschwitz'. In the coming years when I understood 'Auschwitz' more clearly, the comparison of the Jewish massacre in Europe with the massacre during the India–Pakistan Partition did not seem totally disagreeable. Somewhere in the corner of the heart, it does feel meaningful. There was essentially one person to be blamed for Auschwitz: Hitler. It is difficult to blame any one person for the massacre of the Partition. Hindus, Muslims, Sikhs, and the English, all were responsible for it.

Whenever two tragedies are compared, we usually compare their causes. But the truth is, tragedies become great and terrible not because of their causes but their consequences. I say if I've witnessed the Indian Partition, then I've witnessed the Auschwitz of Europe. Furthermore, I say I've witnessed every massacre that has taken place in the world. Because, in the end, all massacres will leave the same images. The ways of dying may be different, but dead bodies will speak the same language. I am a survivor of the Partition. You could see me as a survivor of Auschwitz. All it will take is a little emotional effort.

I know the future generations may not look at this tragedy in the same way as I do; it is quite possible that all will be forgotten after three or four generations, or even if it is remembered and mentioned, the younger generation may simply rebuff it saying, we don't want to smell the buried dead. But someone should tell them that these dead once throbbed with life, that they wrote their life's story using the alphabet of wounds. Someone should tell them—when exile is imposed, it is the soul that gets wounded the most.

All the people who came to Sindhu Library had wounded souls.

There was one Jamna Das, who had lost an eye in childhood—a childhood seared in the riots of Partition. He woke a good three hours before first light, heated oil in a large skillet, and fried nearly 500 poppadoms. They were no ordinary poppadoms but special Sindhi-styled khichiya. He stacked them in a large bamboo basket and sold them in local trains, shunting all day between VT and Kalyan. In the evening, he came to the library and read the papers. He would give the few poppadoms that remained in his basket to Basar Mal, wrapping them first in newspaper.

There was one Heera Nand, who taught mathematics in a nearby school. He carried so much hurt and anger in his heart that Pakistan cropped up in every other sentence he mouthed as a swear word. If he had to go to the loo, he said, 'Wait, let me go to Pakistan and come!' like an expletive exploding in a fit of urgency. And yet, despite all the hatred for Pakistan, he wanted to go there once for the last time, when his end was near, so that his last rites could be performed at the crematorium in Rohri town of Sukkur district, where he had cremated his parents. He wanted his ashes to be immersed, like his ancestors', in the Indus River flowing near Rohri. His dreams would never come true.

And bragging about his bravery every time, there was the dandy Ishwar Chander, too. His hair had turned grey at an early age, on which, now and then, he spattered a layer of henna. As a result, his hair in places flashed blotches of orange. His conversations were peppered with the choicest

Urdu couplets called *sher*. He had a couplet fit for every occasion: Water does not come in the neighbourhood, a *sher* to describe that. Pimples have erupted as a side effect of constipation on his beloved's cheeks, a flowery *sher* for that. No matter on which part of the earth rain fell, in his *sher*, that fresh sweetness always distilled from the earth of his Sindh.

One Hero Lalvani. His desires matched his name. Flushed with vigour, he wanted to become a film hero. For years, he struggled in Bollywood. The longest role he ever got in Hindi films was that of a taxi driver—twelve whole seconds of screen time, yet his face was never once shown. (Lalvani was at the wheel, and the scene was filmed from the backside.) Nevertheless, the spirited fellow always carried a portfolio of his many 'stylish' photographs under his arm; he swanked about the Bollywood tales as if the stars were his personal friends; and he claimed to have seen the legendary star Madhubala's almost rabbit-like 'pure ivory with larger-than-usual nipple' right breast.

There was Ramsinghani too, who sat in the library, in a corner, silently and intently, the whole time. He wouldn't talk to anyone, wouldn't even answer a simple greeting of 'Ram-Ram, Sai'. One often saw him preoccupied with poems of the medieval Sufi Sachal Sarmast. His silence was such that his proximate presence frequently went unremarked. One day, the police came to the library and nabbed him. The next day, one got to know from the papers that he was Haji Mastan's right-hand man. In those days, Mastan was the biggest mafia don, and Ramsinghani had committed eleven barbaric murders for him. At the time of his arrest in the library, a quarter kilo of smuggled gold was found in a cloth bag slung over his shoulder. People were incredulous. Stunned. Such a quiet human but such a savage beast! Ramsinghani's mind had all the time rustled with restlessness; the poetry and spirituality of Sachal Sarmast probably tranquillized his mind——

There were many more. Take one name, ten more names would come to mind. There were enough people.

Give one breath, and a book will live a thousand years. There were enough breaths. The library bloomed. An ancient civilization inhabited these breaths.

So he waits for the people who once came here, treading the endless length between his chair and the window with a kind of unbreakable conviction that does not slacken, despite his footsteps whispering, *'Those who have waited too long should have little hope.'*

Post the Partition, when he had arrived in this city, he would sniff every person coming from Larkana. After shaking hands, he would sniff their palms, closing his eyes, but he could never find in any palm the same fragrance of guava.

* * *

Leaving the books on the floor, he returns to the table. He sniffs his palms. The palms wafted the dampness of the rag.

He looks at the detached book cover lying on the table. Despite being inured to hardships, his heart melted every time a book peered waiflike at him. For years he has been receiving nasty threats, that if he doesn't sell the land of his library—the space where his books dwell—it will be taken from him, that he will be killed: a bullet hole in his temple, poison in his food, or a push from a skyscraper roof.

He wipes the book cover lovingly. Then the book. A library card is stuck on its last page. How many times that blue-coloured card had been stamped! He looks at the date. The book was last issued seventeen years ago. To one Bhagat Ram R. Juneja.

He takes out glue from the drawer and smears it indulgently on the binding, then places the book gently inside the book cover.

'Oh, my sweet child! Why do you sulk so much? There. There. Stay happily now stuck to your book, alright?'

He pats the book compassionately, then reaches for an old-issue register. Postcard-sized calendars of many different years interspace the pages of the register. He pauses at a page. Beyond the page, the register is empty. He reads the date on this last page, goes back to the calendar of the initial pages, and does some calculations. A total of eleven years, four months and twenty-one days had passed without anyone borrowing a book from this library.

5

DIL KHUSH

*'He avoided participation of any kind, never became mixed up
in anything, didn't believe, didn't revolt, and didn't become
disillusioned.'*

—Imre Kertész, *Liquidation*

Further down the library was Dil Khush Sambose wallah's
shop. How and when samosa became sambosa, no one knew.
There was always a throbbing commotion-like atmosphere in
the shop. I don't know if he ever kept a count of how many
people visited his shop throughout the day. With a spoon in
hand, he would be continuously clanging a six-foot metal urn.
The tall urn had a spigot near the bottom. He would put a cup
under the spigot, and piping hot tea would flow into the cup.

The tea had a distinctive local flavour to it. The milk
was not the usual milk; perhaps Dil Khush burnt it in a

particular way. The sweet, heady aroma of half-burnt cream would begin to emanate from his small kitchen as early as five-thirty, even before first light. Making a big plateful, he would keep it covered with a fine muslin cloth next to the kettle. The aroma would waft in all directions. Rust-coloured cream. Like roasted vermicelli. The colour glowed in the yellow light of the streetlamp in the predawn silence. Whatever that special cream was, it was a hit among the autorickshaw fellows around the area.

The Nehru Chowk autorickshaw stand was close by. At any time of the day, at least twenty-five to thirty autos were parked there. And sometimes, the line of autos lengthened to such an extent that the entire street from Nehru Chowk to Dil Khush's shop would be jammed. Just with parking. If the crowd in front of Sambose wallah's grew denser than usual, the scenario would resemble a melee. And if a big car or truck appeared, pandemonium would break out. It was a narrow street, and there was no alternative. The street was also a place of congregation for the unemployed workers. From eight o'clock in the morning, they would start spilling in, and by ten or eleven, the street would convert into a workers' fair; whoever wanted to hire them would start arriving around ten o'clock or so and, after negotiating the rate with the workers in harsh, disparaging voices, take them along. Still, a good twenty to twenty-five workers always remained without work. But this crowd, too, would dwindle as the afternoon drew on. I could never fathom where they dispersed empty-handed!

In Dil Khush Sambose wallah's shop, the item that was least popular was the samosa. He had opened the shop primarily for samosas, but it quickly converted into a tea and vada pav centre. He also stocked cheap candy drops and biscuits, but buyers of these were also few. One thing was in abundance—pictures. All kinds of pictures: all religions, all castes. From Guru Nanak to Lord Satyanarayan. From Jesus Christ to Dattatreya. From Mahatma Gandhi to Indira Gandhi. From Gautama Buddha to Bheemrao Ambedkar. The latest addition was a large newspaper cut-out of Chhatrapati Shivaji.

Whereas Dil Khush Sambose wallah was a Sikh. A Sardar—a *Labana* Sardar. Dil Khush often mentioned during conversations that in business, there was no religion. Rather 'business' was itself the name of a religion. So the idea was to hang in his shop the picture of the one currently trending. If a wave of Dalit Panther rose, then Ambedkar appeared on the walls; if the Sangha wave swept the region, then Lord Rama. Recently, when there were many Shiv Sena fellows among the autorickshaw drivers, Dil Khush hung the picture of Shivaji.

The motto was: Don't get embroiled in any mess at any cost. Jai-jai to this, and jai-jai to that—hail one and all!

Besides, if a particular wave disappeared, he did not take down that picture; it would still adorn the wall of his shop. In this way, he maintained a remarkable goodwill and harmony.

6

MY NAME IS 'I'

'Whatever falls from the sky above, thou shall not curse it. That includes the rain.'

—Elif Shafak, *The Bastard of Istanbul*

Someone is following me.

One day, this weird feeling began to bother me even when there was nothing that could confirm my suspicion. Perhaps it was my overactive imagination. But still, what kind of a fancy was this? Every ten steps I would halt, as if someone's gaze shackled tight my feet.

The girl at the yellow window, who I felt looked like Vermeer's 'Girl with a Pearl Earring', would similarly tie my feet with her gaze, but that window was far off. Then who was watching me, walking step by step behind me?

Abruptly, without stopping, I turned around and saw a familiar figure moving hurriedly out of sight. My eyes had caught the suspect. My forehead wrinkled.

Returning home, I asked my mother, 'Were you in Mossad?'

She was chopping lady's fingers. Without looking up, she asked, 'What do you mean?'

'Why were you following me?' I asked bluntly.

'And why should I follow you?' but the tone of her voice gave away her lie.

'Tell me,' I insisted.

My mother couldn't control her laughter. She laughed like a naughty monkey, while I stared at her like a confused kitten.

'I had come to see that girl,' she said.

I nearly jumped out of my skin. How did she know about the girl at the yellow window? I asked nervously, 'What girl?'

She laughed and, in that shy way of hers, said, 'Arré, that same girl you were telling me about the other day. How her long hair fills your palm . . .'

'OhOhOhhhhh!' I slapped my forehead and slumped onto the sofa, 'What yaar, Ma! Are you really like this? Or do you simply act this way?'

Reproach was in my voice. But it had no effect on her. Her entire being was dancing with joy. She was cajoling me, 'I have to see her. Just once! Okay, show me from afar. I want to see who it is you like so much.'

I grimaced, 'I don't like no one! And don't follow me on the road from now on.'

Saying this, I stomped out. She called after me, but I went and locked myself in my room.

I was, of course, faking anger. Now alone in the room, I blushed, realizing I had a big smile painted on my face. Actually, two days ago, I had boasted to my mother about Imbelo, as if she were a real, living girl. The way I described her long hair, dangling earrings, and charming face, my mother grew curious and wanted to know more about her. She was convinced that I went out with her every day.

I was merely playing with her. Little did I know that she would be so filled with a desire to see Imbelo that she would follow me out into the street. Although, whenever I think of her antic, I feel a loving tenderness towards her.

The next day before leaving the house, I asked her, 'You didn't tell Pau, no?'

She said, 'Let me see her first.'

I said, still keeping my secret from her, 'I'll show you when the time comes. Just, don't tell him.'

'Are you meeting her now?' she asked, seeing me leave.

I continued adding to the lie, 'Yes, yes. She has called me to a library. Can I go now? But don't follow me, please, or else I will quarrel with you on the road itself.'

My mother said, her eyes dancing, 'Then I will tell your Pau.'

I looked at her with big, helpless eyes so that she took pity. At the same time, a new fear struck me that she might also be playing with me. I kept looking back all the way to the library. Thankfully, she was nowhere in sight.

* * *

When for the first time I entered Sindhu Library, I felt intimidated by its dark, damp interiors, mustiness, and its mystery. In the compound outside, a woman sat with balloons in her hand. Balloons in every colour, restless in the breeze, waiting for their release. It had rained a little while ago, and the ground near where she sat was wet. Between her and the wetness, a one-and-a-half-year-old child slept on a gunnysack, covered with a piece of soft blanket. The flies hovered over him, which she kept shooing every so often with her other hand.

A half-eaten vada pav rested on a piece of paper, and flies hovered over that, too.

I felt scared going in. First of all, that balloon woman had made me edgy. Then, there was this dampness inside, which, too, was enough to kindle such feelings. Halting nervously at the door itself, I viewed the dank interior. The books were all over the floor. The racks were empty. In their overwhelming emptiness, one could not so much as feel the books' presence. Beyond the emptiness, there were more racks. Emptiness again in them. Beyond that emptiness, another emptiness—that sat taking shelter of the wall. On the left side, there were chairs, and a table with many more balding books on it. A thermos lay open. To one side of the table, a sandbag on the ground served as an improvised footboard. There was no such thing as a floor—or it may have existed once. Now there were pits in many places and attempts to tamp down cement over them. At one time it had probably been sheathed with linoleum, for its marks still lingered. Some lino pieces that could escape total deracination clung, even now, in the corners where the wall met the floor. A fan hung above. Grime sat on its edges and the place that housed the motor had become yellow in embarrassment. Beyond the chair, a tube light shone with cobwebs hanging from its choke strip. A sheeted, thin mattress was spread on the floor, a pillow on one side, a bolster on the other. The kind of fresh creases the sheet bore showed that somebody had just risen from there.

I can never forget that ghostly silence of the library.

In a library, even otherwise, spirits rove—of great writers, old books, torn bindings, half-hearted librarians, broken furniture, toiling termites, and sauntering roaches.

I went and stood near the table. There were two empty chairs facing it. After waiting a while longer, I sat down in one of the chairs.

The sound of someone walking from behind the bookracks put me on my feet again. I stood listening to the footsteps. An old, doddering man emerged around the corner of the rack, taking extremely slow steps. I saw he was wearing flip flops over socks. His kurta was like a shirt—it had the cut of a kurta, but the length of a shirt. The pyjamas were like that of old times. Wide-leg bottom. As if a pair of loose and light pants had been stitched from shirt material. Most of his hair was gone. Nose sharp, albeit a little crooked. Eyes glazed in thick-framed glasses. Such people didn't cross my path often. But whenever they did, I mimicked and mocked them. Looking at this man, I had an urge to do the same, once again.

He saw me and halted in his tracks. Then slowing came around the table and sat in his chair.

The evening had darkened. A cool breeze was blowing in from outside. Along with a few raindrops. Either it was raining, or it was a preparation for the rain to come. I thought of the balloon woman sitting outside.

'I had come here once or twice during the day, but it was closed.'

'Library opens only in the evenings. You did not read the timings?'

'Where are the timings written?'

'On the board outside.'

I kept quiet.

'But, of course,' he himself retracted after a moment, 'the timings have rubbed off.'

He bent down behind the table. I peeked over to see he had changed into shoes and was tying the laces. With pyjamas, he had worn white sports shoes.

'Five to seven is the timing. And now it is seven. Do you want to meet someone, or has anyone sent you with a message?'

'No. I was passing by and caught sight of the board, so I came in.'

I went to the window. From here, that yellow window was clearly visible. But presently, I did not perceive any movement there. I went to the books. Many were rotting. Beyond the racks, the space stretched far inside, elongating slowly into silence and emptiness——

'May I?'

I did not wait for his answer and went into the spacious length; it was longer than I had imagined. My interest for this place had been growing. One could erect a grand film set here, I thought.

There were some more old chairs, either an arm or a leg—something or the other—was broken. Across the racks, on the far side, a broken stove was kept. There was a jar, in which sugar had turned dust-coloured. A few stove pins lay scattered. And the wall bore soot marks from the burning of a kerosene stove. Over the soot, someone had placed their hand, and its imprint shone distinctly. Next to it was a window and then a bathroom.

The old man had gotten ready to leave. He had closed his sling bag. The thermos had gone inside it.

In his eyes, there were no questions for me. There was no curiosity. There were no answers either. There was something akin to the emptiness that lay scattered in the racks. Emptiness that told something would have been here once. The light would have come slanting quietly through the door and got lost in the expanse of the labyrinth inside. From here, a voice would have felt anxious to sneak outside. Can I recognize the marks of the voices pecked on the walls, windows, and doors?

'Can I have a book?'

'Why?'

'To read . . .'

'Come tomorrow at five, you can take a membership then.'

His abrupt manner would have, looking at the deserted bleakness of the place, infuriated anyone. I wanted to stop him and haul him over the coals. Why on earth had he opened the shop then? But much as I wanted, I could neither rebuke nor mock him.

I came out with him. He bent down and padlocked the door.

The balloon woman was still sitting in the same place. She had tied her balloons to a nail in the wall. The child sleeping beside her had woken up. She was feeding him the half-eaten vada pav that had lain on the paper before.

The old man stopped abruptly. For a moment, he gazed at the swaying balloons. Then, putting extra pressure on the cane, hobbled slowly out.

The woman, sliding her gunnysack along, started moving towards a dry place.

7

THE OLD WOMAN IS SILENT

'Beneath the onion's dry and crackly outer skin we find another, more moist layer, that once detached, reveals a third, beneath which a fourth and fifth wait whispering. And each skin sweats words too long muffled, and curlicue signs, as if a mystery-monger from an early age, while the onion was still germinating, had decided to encode himself.'

—Günter Grass, *Peeling the Onion*

People called her Mangan's Ma, so it is understandable that her son's name would be Mangan. But no one knew where Mangan was. No one had seen Mangan. In fact, it was not in anyone's memory to recall that yes, there was a lad named Mangan, who while playing cricket in the neighbourhood had broken someone's window pane, that his catapult had wounded so-and-so's forehead, that he once was so small that he had peed on such-and-such grandpa or granduncle, that when he grew up a little bit more, his vulnerable toddle had been watched with such fondness. Mangan was nowhere. Mangan was no one. There was just Mangan's Ma.

Mangan's Ma was very wrinkled, with a weird toothless mouth. She was skeletal, so much so that she sensed danger even from a breeze. She mostly wore a long pink tunic and wide-leg Shikarpur pyjamas. And with this, flip flops. She always covered her head with a veil. Thick-framed soda-bottle spectacles sat on her face. Her so-called beard had three finger-length grey strands that dangled, and two of these often coiled up to nestle against her chin.

She had such a craze for cleanliness that it had become a habit for her to wash everything. She not only washed vessels and clothes, not just the floor and footwear, but every other day, the walls of the house too. She would wash all the furniture. If her food was hot, she would eat, else if the roti went cold, she would wash it too, dipping it once in water and put it to dry under the fan, and even before it dried, dunk it in dal and munch it off. She had not yet understood the technique of washing cooked vegetables but coins, notes, framed-unframed pictures, all were washed before they could be used. Many times, Basar Mal had seen her washing even the switchboard. In her heedless doggedness to wipe the switches with a wet cloth, she had tasted one too many electric shocks. Because her hands constantly played with water, the skin of her fingertips had eternally turned white.

She had similar feelings for water. People said Mangan's Ma's thirst was unquenchable. In those localities, water was supplied at a fixed time and people filled all the water required during that time. But Mangan's Ma could be seen anytime at the locality's municipal tap, at the hand pump, holding an old iron bucket or a plastic jerry can. At any time, she could knock at your door and ask in Sindhi, '*Dis th putra, paani aayo aa chha?*' (Just see, son, has the water come?)

'*Na amma, paani achi kare vayo. Haane na eendo. Subaane acho tavaan.*' (No amma, water came, but it has gone already. It won't come now. You come tomorrow.)

'*Hut, muaa Chandraa. Charayo.*' (Move, you dead cunning rascal. You crackpot.)

Mumbling thus, Mangan's Ma would return, but it is quite probable that the following day, she could ask you the same question.

Today, as always, Basar Mal had explained that the water tank of the house was full, that they didn't need any more water, but her soundless gaze had silenced him, and she had gone about depositing her jerry cans and water kegs carefully near the door.

When he got down from the autorickshaw, he found Mangan's Ma squatting, in the afternoon's lull, at the hand pump. The jerry can was brimming. Mangan's Ma, exhausted from the constant pushing of the pump's handle, had wanted to rest for a couple of minutes before she could lug her jerry can back.

He went and stood near her. Mangan's Ma lifted her face and looked at him. With the same gentle unsmiling

vacuity. After gazing at Basar Mal, she let her gaze
wander to the filled can. Then, placing her hands on her
knees tried to get up. Basar Mal put his stick in Mangan's
Ma's hands, picked up the jerry can, and started walking
ahead.

Basar Mal cannot remember when Mangan's Ma
acquired this penchant for washing everything. He cannot
remember when she started feeling insecure about water.
He also cannot remember the last time Mangan's Ma spoke
anything to him.

To Basar Mal Jetharam Purswani, she appears like an
onion whose outer skin is dry but, with every peeling,
reveals one more moist and soft skin. An onion that has
deferred her peeling. Who has wrapped herself in another
skin to save the secret words encoded inside. Not a sound
flows out from inside the numerous doors of the onion.
Bound in these circumvolutions, perhaps it is the captivity
of the inside that she cannot unfetter—to emerge from
where she has forgotten the mantra of Simsim. It is quite
possible that Basar Mal has himself forgotten the mantra
required to enter the space inside.

He recalls a bygone afternoon when coming back on
foot from the station, Mangan's Ma, whom he called Jalo
then, had demanded, stamping her feet, 'Enough! I can't
walk anymore. Carry me in your arms.' In response, Basar
Mal had simply peeped into Jalo's eyes, and she had burst
into a peal of delightful giggles.

He always loved the arcs of black kohl under her eyelids. He would say they held the dreams of her eyes. When a little kohl streaked to her temples, he would tease, 'Jalo, watch out! Your dreams are floating away.' That same night, he remembers, after finishing dinner at home, they had impulsively wandered off and sucked endlessly on mango popsicles that their lips stained yellow and their clothes, too, from the front, which they discovered to their wild merriment on returning home. In the name of her laughter, Basar Mal remembers that smiling-giggling face.

And he remembers the evening she had shown up at Sindhu Library for the first time. How can he forget that long-ago evening? Only a few months earlier, he had started Sindhu Library. She came, and won everyone's heart with her melodious voice and scholarly attitude.

A smile grows young on Basar Mal's old lips, 'No, not like this, Basar Mal! Remember it with a little more love in your old heart.'

He closes his eyes to concentrate on that part of his life which, for him, was something like life lived, something like an enchanting story found in books.

Basar Mal knew Jalo from childhood. She lived in Shikarpur. Their fathers were best friends. A warm, easy-going relationship existed between the families. Jalo, seven years older than Basar Mal, would boss over him. When she turned nineteen, she was married, and she went away.

A few years later, Basar Mal fell in love with Jaam, lost her, wandered dangerously in search of her, failed miserably, and then, somehow crossing the border, he came to India and found a job in Mumbai.

Then one day, while wandering around Flora Fountain looking for books, his eyes fell on Jalo's elder brother, Deader. He didn't know his real name; he had dubbed him 'Deader' (which in Sindhi meant frog) because of his frog-like eyes. They were both overjoyed to see each other, but they were probably more astonished than happy. Years after the Partition, if you meet an old friend from your own Sindh in not-so-your-own Mumbai, then, naturally, you will become a creature of emotions. Deader dragged Basar Mal home, and there he saw Jalo. True, he had forgotten her over the years, but she came back looking exactly like the old Jalo. Basar Mal was meeting her after about ten years, but it seemed as if, like the age-old profundities, time had little effect on her.

Deader told him about her life's injustices, and how disaster came upon her. After marriage, she had left Shikarpur to live with her husband in Lahore. Then in the Partition riots, a stick-wielding man had broken her husband's head.

Basar Mal still remembers the intimate pain with which Jalo contributed to the story—

The entire street coloured red. Looking at her husband's dead body, she fell unconscious. She was in hospital on regaining consciousness, and the nurses didn't let her go to the Anarkali bazaar square, where her husband's bloody body had lain. By the time she was discharged from the hospital, the Anarkali bazaar had been completely shut down, the dead bodies had been removed from the street, and the water-bearers pouring water from their leather carriers had wiped out all traces of blood. Wretched Jalo! She could never get to know who had killed her husband. Was it another death in the riot, or had someone ambushed and killed him? What happened to his dead body in just three days? Was he even cremated or not?

She ran to government offices, went to police stations, inquired in hospitals, but his body was nowhere to be found. How could she find it? The Lahore of 1947 was no longer a city but a historical morgue. Every day, so many were slaughtered that the crematoriums to burn them and cemeteries to bury them were insufficient. At every opportunity, the government employees would pick up the dead bodies from the streets, load them in the truck, and throw them in pits outside the city. And on paper they would write 'The mass funeral was duly performed.'

If Jalo had stayed any longer, she, too, would have been slayed. It was difficult to walk through the streets. Death lay in wait at every street corner. She somehow reached her brother's place in Shikarpur, and from there, they came to Mumbai. Her life changed. She shut herself in a room, speaking only to a few people, meeting even fewer.

Basar Mal remembers the happiness on her face on seeing him. Deader said he hadn't seen her laugh with so much feeling in a long time! Basar Mal remembers her room in Kalbadevi, with books all over her bed.

'You sleep with books?' he asked her, smiling. His old mischief returned on seeing Jalo.

'Yes, a dervish told me, whatever I've lost, I'll find in books,' she answered, smiling back at him.

'This is amazing! A dervish had told me the same thing,' Basar Mal said, greatly astonished, hearing which Jalo laughed so much and with such delight that Basar Mal understood that she didn't believe him.

Confused, he stuttered, 'Arré, really! A dervish told me. Really.'

Since then, whenever Basar Mal mentioned dervish, Jalo would laugh her delightful unpretentious laughter. His entire life Basar Mal kept making her believe, and her entire life Jalo kept believing that Basar Mal had merely said it to flirt with her.

He remembers when he invited her to his library, the way Jalo laughingly ignored the invite, Basar Mal felt she wouldn't come, but after a few days, she dropped in on him with her brother.

There were many people in the library that day, and the talk among them was of Sindh, as usual. The conversation turned to Shah Abdul Latif and his book *Risalo*, when suddenly Jalo, in her utterly sweet and shy voice, started singing what the heroine Moomal sang in the book calling out her lover Rana:

Aao Rana, rahu raat
Tuhinje chaangey khe chandan chaariyaan
Ratiyaan deehaan rooh mein, tan tuhinje jee taat
Aao Rana, rahu raat
Tuhinje chaangey khe chandan chaariyaan

(Come, Rana, stay the night with me
I will feed your camel sandalwood
as fodder
Night and day, in me, in my soul,
I want you
Come, Rana, stay the night with me
I will feed your camel sandalwood
as fodder)

Jalo sang while Basar Mal's eyes filled. He desperately tried to hide his tears. But one thing he could not hide even from himself, and that was Jaam's face. He felt it was not Jalo but Jaam singing. That same voice, same poetry, same Shah Abdul Latif, same Moomal, same Rana, but a different girl, an altered boy.

When the song got over, a mesmerized Basar Mal held Jalo's hand. The aroma of guava descended all around the two of them, perhaps travelling from his past.

Outside, it had grown dark. The last visitors had left after an all-evening discussion and celebration of the past. Deader was still sitting on the chair in the back and, holding hands, Jalo and Basar Mal on the chairs nearby. They would have sat like that, silent and unmoving, like a sculpture in the middle of a garden, had Deader not interrupted them.

That day, it was as if God played a melodious accelerando on the piano of their lives to prophesy. Because a few days later in the library, breaking a long, awkward silence between them, Basar Mal had innocently, without context or setting, tossed a strangely-framed question to Jalo:

'Can I come into your life?'

'No, thanks. It's a complete wreck already.'

The alacrity with which Jalo whipped out an answer had Basar Mal reeling first in amazement, then in admiration of her wit and sense of humour. After that, they lapsed into another long silence, smiling into their books and exchanging furtive glances.

How they made each other happy! Her childhood mischiefs, arrogance, and bossiness all returned after their marriage. She was full of dreams and singing, a spirited woman who could not only sing but explain with great erudition all of Shah's lines.

Basar Mal also remembers the night when Jalo had wailed aloud, hiccupping in his lap on the bed, and in frustration, continually asked him, 'Why wouldn't this Mangan arrive after all?'

'*Eendo, Jalo, eendo. Mangan eendo hekado diyan. Chav Jhulelal.*' (He will arrive, Jalo, he will arrive. Mangan will arrive one day. Take the name of Jhulelal.)

And she had said weeping, 'You know, my brother Deader says I must have winked at misfortune, and that's why misfortune like a stray street lover keeps following me.'

That night Basar Mal had acutely felt that life is nothing but a gold-rimmed darkness.

For a long time, they had both remained silent, drowning in themselves. Jalo would, at intervals, place her hand on her belly. Raising her tunic, look at the belly. Closing her eyes, write something on Basar Mal's palm. *When would this*

Mangan arrive? From the next morning, Basar Mal started calling her not Jalo but Mangan's Ma. Whenever he uttered 'Mangan's Ma', Jalo's eyes would brighten, then fill, then go into a vacuousness and get stuck there. With each utterance, the sensation of Mangan's being would deepen. The hope of his coming into this world would become verdant. Gradually, even the entire neighbourhood started calling her Mangan's Ma.

How long has it been since she covered herself with another skin to bury deep inside, shrinking her language to just an unspoken, unexpressed desire, a foundling of a dream that sits at her heart's edge, making its overpowering presence unbearable—that one day her Mangan will come into this world?

There are many things Basar Mal does not remember.

Yet many he remembers often.

Mangan's Ma does not speak. Basar Mal remembers her delightful giggles.

Mangan's Ma remains silent. Basar Mal remembers her mischievous merriment.

Mangan's Ma, head bent, washes a baby guitar. Basar Mal remembers Mangan's non-arrival.

8

THE BOOK
COVER TELLS A TALE

'When the child was a child, it didn't know that it was a child. To
it, everything had a soul, and all souls were one.'
—Peter Handke, *Song of Childhood*

I am that torn book cover Basar Mal set aside for mending.

The day he was pulling out Shah Abdul Latif's Sindhi
love ballad 'Sassi-Punnu', another book, ripe and heavy,
had softly plopped onto the floor. It was this library's oldest
book. The most senile book. Which always goes unnoticed
anyway. Have you ever gone to a library? If yes, then, have
you ever pondered which would be the oldest book in
there? Have you ever felt like seeking that oldest book? And
reading it? Or even patting it? Or stroking it? For some few
fleeting moments, glimpsing it?

Such thoughts do not usually pop into one's mind. I am a book, and as a matter of fact, it is I who have saved the story of the earliest human ancestors. But would a human know the world's first book? Does it even survive? Very unlikely. You see, no human saved that book.

And why would humans want to save books when they don't even save each other? The extent of their desire to ravage and devastate, pursue and possess is beyond all imaginable limits. Wanting to assert their lordship, when nations and cultures and societies and communities attack one another, they first target the women, next the books. From this perspective, one sadly finds that both women and books share a common plight. Do you know when language originated, 'book' was a masculine word? Even in those times, it was accepted that books were the source of knowledge, and since the entire knowledge singularly belonged to men of the society, the book was masculine. It was given the revered status of a guru. Then the books were attacked, and they couldn't protect themselves. Those who cannot protect themselves are gradually feminine-gendered inside the language. All conspiracies are hatched inside the language entirely. All deliberations of the state are coldly etched within.

I am fond of Basar Mal. I am fond of every person that reads books, keeps books, loves books. Works of art and literature are an affirmation of our inner strengths. The act of creation is an act of defying death. As I am saying this, a story of the Sama Veda leaps to mind. It is in the

'Chhandogya' Upanishad, a text filled with lilting rhythms, hymns, and mantras:

Once Death was after the gods. The gods panicked. They had to escape Death—go hide somewhere. Go, but where to go? Hide, but where to hide? Death would reach them everywhere. Short of breath and ideas, they snuck into the Vedas and covered themselves with *chhand* or verse. It is interesting to note that the word '*chhand*' is derived from the root word '*chhandas*,' meaning cover or camouflage. So, the gods covered themselves with poetry and escaped from Death.

The sages of the Upanishads say poetry or *chhand* saves us from a bad death. When all the negativity comes headlong towards us, the verse like an umbrella will shield us. What a beautiful thing to say in praise of poetry! It is said deeper the understanding of death in a language or culture, the finer the poetry written in it.

I find myself nodding in approval to our tradition that links immortality with literature. For Basar Mal, books are so much a part of him, that away from them, he would be as good as dead. I know Basal Mal felt very sad when he accidentally dropped that oldest book of his library. He had let out an anguished cry, as if by his negligence he had dropped his own child. I—who bound the book and kept it safe all these years—separated in the process. Basar Mal gingerly lifted the book and tried to shove it gently inside me but I tore. He kept me aside thinking he would soon stick me back to my book. Subsequently, some books he stuck with gum and returned to their places, but I, not among those, remained unglued.

Separated from my book, and displaced. Waiting to be joined, and whole again.

Basar Mal has forgotten me as one forgets oneself.

My plight is like that of Chakwa and Chakwi. Have you heard the tale of Chakwa-Chakwi? They were two handsome birds, two ruddy sheldrakes. They would fly together, make merry, rubbing wing against wing make heat. There was much love in their togetherness. Playfully, one day, they disrupted a saint's meditation and incurred his wrath. They were condemned to pass the night apart from each other, on opposite banks of the river. There was much love in this separation too. The whole night, every night, Chakwa perched on one shore trilled mournful poems of their pains of love, while Chakwi susurrated restlessly on the other shore, but despite the craving, they couldn't seek togetherness. They prayed all night to be freed of the saint's curse, but the saint had vanished without a trace. Say, a dark curse that befell love, has it ever been recalled?

The night that has befallen them is an interminable one. Still, they wait in hope that the two banks would join. I'm like the Chakwa-Chakwi pair. I'm here as a book cover while my book lies elsewhere. And while Basar Mal sits patiently here, his wait stands across some forgotten river.

Look at me a little closer, you will see my face looking like Basar Mal's—

Each of us is incomplete in some corner of the world: an infinite limitless world that is itself incomplete, without beginning or end.

Without beginning or end. Life and art exist in this incompleteness. Any thought, any art will come and go, unescorted by conception or completion. No one knows from where one came, where one will go—what is known is the in-between.

Yet what do we do? We supply a start and end point. Why? Because our intellect desires to view a thing in a particular start-finish way for appeasement or convenience.

If I am mended, will I be complete?

Will Basar Mal, if he finds his beginning?

We keep making, we keep breaking, we keep drawing, we keep erasing, that we are our own lamps, we keep lighting, we keep annihilating. One day, when we exhaust our ingenuity to make ourselves complete, tired of the efforts or otherwise, we convince ourselves that we are complete. This is a game we play with ourselves.

Do you know excellent art never runs after completeness? It doesn't have fixed essences. Take, for example, the ballad of 'Sassi-Punnu', my charming companion who I shelved with till I fell down: The 'Sassi-Punnu' story is complete, the way we view something as complete. But this classic tale keeps progressing towards incompleteness: their love is incomplete and their meeting and their separation and the intrigues of the royal family and Sassi's death and Punnu's wailing. An incompleteness that is not at the level of events but feelings. An incompleteness that is not a linguistic operation but a sensory experience, invalidating the beginning and the ending. An imagined incompleteness in all its fineness. And an imagined completeness. The half-sunk swaying veil. The story of 'Sassi-Punnu' is always complete and always incomplete.

My poet Sahir says,

A tale which is difficult to be brought to an end
It's good to give it a beautiful twist and leave.

In our own stories, perhaps we should look for that beautiful turn, because we do not know how we'll finish. Nobody does. Neither Basar Mal nor the Chakwa-Chawi nor I.

9

DIL KHUSH

'We do not inherit this land from our ancestors; we borrow it from our children.'

A Haida Indian saying

'Tell me, can this shop be displaced after being here for twenty years?' Dil Khush Sambose wallah asks me. I don't say anything. I simply watch him smear the red dry garlic chutney on the vada. I don't know how many times he clangs on the six-foot urn. Clang—clang—clang! It seems as if he is ringing a school bell announcing 'School is dismissed'.

'Tell me, can someone move it out?' he asks again.

'Who is removing you from here?' I hold out my plate to him, 'Here, put some wet chutney.'

'No one . . .' And he goes silent. From a ceramic jar, he splatters green chutney on the vada. A few blobs of the chutney fall on my shirt. I shoot Dil Khush an angry glare, but by then, he's again become engrossed in clanging his metal tea urn. I take out my handkerchief to wipe off the blobs. In the afternoons, his shop is less crowded. The reason, he offers, is that during the daytime, people eat proper food, and not fast food like samosa and tea. At this hour of the day, only such people stop by who want to make do with their grub by consuming samosa and tea.

While wiping the gooey blobs off my shirt, I give him another glare, and he bursts out laughing. This Sardar's head, nestled between a smallish turban and a long beard, seems so big that many times I feel he belongs to some otherworldly species. I feel as if he's landed on Earth in a flying saucer to saunter along with his other mates, and in their excitement and hurriedness and confusion, they've left him behind. And then, to mingle with the people here, he has worn a Sardar's turban. When I see the shape of his laughter hedged by a salt-and-pepper beard, this feeling grows deeper.

'Dil Khush, have you ever felt that your customers love you?'

Posing a question like this to the sort of shopkeeper he is, seems silly. Still, he bothers to return an answer: 'Has any customer of mine ever felt that I love them?' And dinging his urn hard, he starts laughing. I laugh, too, more at his mannerism than his words.

I ask him about the old man of the library. Dil Khush considers him a cynic. This has been my impression, too, since yesterday. He tells me that the old man has looked the same for the past twenty years. Even twenty years ago, he seemed this old. Then, he used to think, maybe twenty years hence the old man would look younger, but twenty years later, that is now, he still has the same oldness.

'Curse that oldie, doesn't get any younger, dammit,' guffaws Dil Khush, sounding his urn once again enthusiastically.

In between packing a takeaway vada pav for a customer, clinking-clanking the cash-drawer, sounding the tea urn, and laughing uproariously, with numerous such interruptions, he manages to tell me about the old man: that he is Sindhi—that in the past, his library had plenty of members—that it bustled with their conversations—that the place is spacious—that in that vast space, he has filled useless trash—that God knows how he makes a living—that earlier he had a job in a bank—that even then he would open his shop only in the evenings—that he shows his anger when I call his library a shop—that I have asked him several times to rent out a small portion of his shop to me—that I find my kitchen space rather small—that in the past, I would voluntarily send him tea in the evenings—that I had told him he was not helping me despite my repeated entreaties—that if he gave me a little bit of his land, would his library close down?—that he would in fact earn some extra dough— that on hearing this, he had become so aggressive he told me to get out—that I stopped sending him the evening tea ever since—that I had never taken money from him for the tea—that he is so elderly that he automatically commands respect—that I hardly see anyone going to him now— that

only one or two oldies visit him sometimes— that this . . .
that that . . . that . . . that . . .

'I have seen his place,' I tell him.

'Then? See? How much unused space is with him?
Simply he has left it hanging!'

'Why do you need that space?'

'For the kitchen. If my kitchen goes there, then in
the shop, I will get a little more space. Then, I can do the
seating inside the shop, no? Then, I can even go for some
renovation.'

'Then, what does he say?'

'What will he say? He did not give it. He said, don't
snatch it, this land is my children's.'

'How many children he has?'

'Arré, none he has! He will die with this land tied to his
throat. The waste paper that's stacked inside—those rotten
books—he calls them his daughters! Has an imaginary child
too, who was never born.'

I wanted to ask him about the girl who kept standing
among the yellow shutters, yellow flower mesh, and
yellow curtains—that her face wore no expression—that
the way she had looked at the muck on my pants, I could
still feel her eyes on me—that these days I pass by that
house looking out for her—that I find the girl always at the
window, her two hands clutching the grille—that it seems
as if she is standing behind the bars of a prison cell—that if
you peered at her face carefully, you would see a silence,
despair, and wait.

I wanted to ask him, who is that girl . . .

Instead I blurt out, 'Who is evicting you from here?'

From where he stands, he is shouting his anger at his servant inside. He turns sharply and looks at me. On his face, there is now an odd graveness—the kind anyone could become intimidated by. On the metal tea urn, his spoon starts coming furiously down. With the resounding clang—clang—clang—clang the whole street begins to resonate, this sound becoming even more deafening than the urn's.

10

MY NAME IS 'I'

'. . . the people were settling themselves for the night, rolling their cloaks for pillows and lying down to rest in the dirty straw. They lay fully-dressed, as if prepared to leave at any moment and continue their journey.'

—Pär Lagerkvist, *The Death of Ahasuerus*

I had not seen a library before this. In the name of a library, my knowledge was limited to those push carts, or old *raddi* paper and scrap shops where we could find comics, magazines, and a few bestsellers. The only reading I'd done was as a young boy. The school where I studied did not have a library. The college I went to had a library, but I shied away from it like a disease. So I never ventured beyond its reading room. I would read either on the computer screen or taking printouts off the net. And that was that.

Never printed books. In college, I would read textbooks, but only the pages I thought were useful for exams. And which pages were useful, either the lecturer told us or the photocopy fellow, who was in great demand among those who regarded classes as something to be actively avoided. That was the breadth of my reading.

But for some time now, my desire to read has returned. I had opposed my Pau, for years, by giving up on books outside my syllabus. I've begun to feel that I should do away with this childish form of opposition. Even if I resumed reading, I could still continue my dissent. However, I don't want to admit it to anyone. Like everything else, I want to keep it a secret.

That's why I was surprised with myself when I asked the old man if I could borrow a book! Suddenly I wanted to read not one or two but many books. Looking at the books in the library, I wanted to ask the old man whether he had read all the books, whether he remembered all of their names? When soft copies could be created of all these books and kept in a small hard drive, why let books occupy so much space?

I wonder who reads books. Whom are they written for? When the old man is not around, what do these books do? When he drapes himself motionless over his chair, do these books watch him? During the old man's absence, do these books move out of their places? Do they still wear their bindings and book covers, or wriggle out of them and, like house sparrows, flap and shake dust and termites off their bodies? Do they sway to a tune? Or sing a song even? On which rhythm do the books dance? On which raga do the books sing?

I don't stop at Dil Khush Sambose wallah's shop. It would be very crowded at this hour. I go past, further down. Towards Central Hospital. Then beyond, towards Farver Line. The cell phone in my pocket beeps an SMS. It is Nikki with one of her old, tiresome 'Santa-Banta' jokes. Without bothering to read, I mechanically type a colon, hyphen and closed bracket. :-) Funny. Happy. And send it to her. And drop the cell phone back into my pocket. I know she'll heat up.

I'd read somewhere that a great many angels descend from the heavens to a ground occasionally to dance all night. They take off their wings. Remove their crowns, switch off the shimmering halo of light round their heads, and dance. They dance with great abandon that, at first sight, appears like a celebration, although from the inside, they are all immensely sad and nurse a desire to take revenge against someone. But the constraint of being an angel forces them to distance themselves from exhibiting such immoral thoughts. So, they dance, suppressing their feelings—a strange, helpless dance— and pretend a celebration.

Do books dance similarly? To the tune of mourning? To the beats of despair? To the rhythm of neglect? Do they, like those angels, smother their feelings and pretend a celebration?

I don't go beyond Central Hospital. I bear the stigma of being born in this government hospital two decades ago. Not once have I gone there after that, despite passing by it often. When my Pau was admitted here, thankfully, I wasn't in town; otherwise, I'd be wondering even then—most unwilling as I always am to enter this morbid place—if I should be beside him. I had questioned him on my return: whether he found only this hospital in the entire city each and every time?

The way I question him often. Critical and harsh. Born of youthful shame.

In college, I was ashamed that I didn't know English and looked for an excuse for not attending classes. I questioned my father whether there wasn't a single English medium school in the entire city that, from grade one to ten, he made me mug my lessons in Hindi? That he wanted me to become an expert in English but didn't send me to an English medium school?

My Pau doesn't give me answers.

'No father has answers to his son's questions,' he says, putting forth his helplessness, 'If questions start troubling a son's heart, then there's a shortcoming in his upbringing.'

After that, my Pau gets up and fumbles about, sometimes checking the electricity metre, sometimes the water motor. Ma consoles me, 'A lot many people don't know English, still they are studying, they are earning. Why do you worry? One day, even your time will come.' And I resolve not to ever speak with them about my upbringing.

But I also don't want to crawl in the rut grooved by an unfair life. I don't want to struggle quietly like Ma. I have often heard stories of her hardships in life when unemployment had hit the family, years of wandering, dragging their belongings along from place to place, from one obscurity to another. I also remember what she told me a couple of years back.

'I had left home when I was pregnant with you,' she said that day, 'You know why? Because of your Pau. His moral discourses, everyday anger, and advice. His jealousies and imposed restrictions. He would never talk about another life growing inside me but would lose no chance to lecture on my shortcomings: "Why haven't you covered your head?" "Why have you switched on the light during the day?" "Why do you have to laugh in front of him?" Finding fault with every activity, every mannerism of mine.

One day, I couldn't bear it anymore. I bundled some clothes and vessels and left his place. Such a big city! I did not know the streets or the language. I had come here only a year before, on marrying your Pau. Somehow, I reached Dadar station. You know how the station is, so many platforms with so many trains, stopping and moving every second, people getting on and off in droves. I was so confused—which train should I board? Who should I ask for help? That day, heaving my bundle of poverty on my head and you in my womb, I struggled from platform number one to nine. I walked to the front, then walked back, over and over, not knowing if the next train would take me home. Home? What home? I laughed. How ironical! As soon as I had left home, I wondered which train would go home. The hell we run away from, our thoughts will, unknowingly or otherwise, search for ways to reach that hell again. There was no train that went home.

Nervous and exhausted, I went to sit on the bench near the newspaper shop on platform one. When I'd come to Mumbai for the first time, your Pau had sat me lovingly on the same bench and from the nearby stall bought me vada pav. I loved it so much that I ate five of them. Since then, I kept asking him to take me to Dadar station for vada pav. I want to laugh at the thought of it now, because when others asked their husbands to take them to Juhu Beach or Chowpatty, I asked him to take me to a platform.

I had lost all count of time, sitting dazed and lost on the bench, when I heard your Pau calling my name. I still remember that quaver in his voice, that tremble of his hand. As you know, the platform is right near the entry, and so Pau would have seen me as soon as he entered the station. He sat on the ground with a thud of relief, looking unfamiliar with his shut mouth and questioning, scared eyes. All of a sudden, he began sobbing while I merely sat motionless like a statue. But I loved the fact that he had actually come searching for me; perhaps he cared for me and remembered that particular memory of love attached to the place! He had somehow guessed the place I could most probably be found.

I quietly returned home with him. The next day, he asked me if I didn't feel scared at the thought of getting lost in the city. Your Pau might have forgotten the question as soon as he asked it, but it stayed with me, and I realized that I had been lost from before—from the time I had come to this house. And now, since another heart beat inside my body, I had no choice but to be lost once again within the four walls of the house. I kind of shut myself off after that. Perhaps your Pau shut himself off too. He stopped his lectures. And since then, we have just been living . . . well . . . like you see now.'

Then she smiled, 'Not since I came back home have I talked so much,' and she never referred to this sad little 'me-in-her-womb' story again.

My running away from Pau is a habit acquired in the womb, I suppose. I don't know if a habit this old can be mended. All I know is, for now, I have to fix myself up, fast.

Tearing a piece of roti, I often contemplate hibernating inside a jar of stored pickles. The day I come out, I'd have turned delicious and useful. I feel like making a smiley again . . . :-)

I stop at Balaji Tea Stall for a smoke, and try to take my mind off all the oldies in my life. Again and again, that yellow window sneaks into my thoughts. On a reflex, I peek behind to check on my trousers. Oho! So the splatter's there even today, but until now, hasn't she seen this splatter? I cackle at my own stupid fantasy. As if she stood there at the window only to look at the muck on my pants! I've seen her several times at the window since that rainy day. And on several occasions, I've halted right in front of it. She has begun to recognize me now. But why hasn't she smiled even once? Doesn't her face look yellow among the yellow shutters and curtains?

My cell phone beeps again. Nikki has responded to my smiley with another smiley. A droopy smiley. :-(Frowning, little moue. Great. I won't keep her in my life now. Now, she'll remain only in my Inbox.

Indeed, I don't like to recall, or keep in memory, people who have exited. Their life or mine. You could consider me deficient in memory if you like. I forget easily. I, in fact, like to forget. I feel the majority of our moments in life are unimportant. To be disregarded and forgotten. That's why it is intolerably irritating when people keep harping about their past. That's why I have this constant friction with my father when he boasts—at your age, I had done this much, earned so much.

One day I snap back, exasperated: 'Pau, stop trumpeting in front of me. The salary you'll retire with would be what I shall get at the time of joining.'

'How? Tell me, how?' he scoffs.

'Don't bother about it. Getting a three to four lakh package is no big deal.' And as always, after such a conversation, either he stalks out of the room in a huff, or I do.

While returning, I see a commotion in front of Dil Khush Sambose wallah's shop. It looks to me more like a free-for-all.

11

THE OLD MAN'S STORY

'When I was little, my ambition was to grow up to be a book.
Not a writer. People can be killed like ants. Writers are not hard
to kill either. But not books: however systematically you try to
destroy them, there is always a chance that a copy will survive and
continue to enjoy a shelf-life in some corner on an out-of-the-way
library somewhere . . .'

—Amos Oz, *A Tale of Love and Darkness*

The pencil annoys him.

When he thinks it is all nice and pointy, right then something happens that the tip breaks and lodges itself in the sharpener. Tapping and patting the sharpener, he somehow removes the broken bit and begins to sharpen afresh.

He reclines against the wall, a drawing book sprawled on his lap, making several lines all over the page, holding the pencil and paper at different angles in his old trembling hand.

Mangan's Ma comes into the room with slow, measured steps, an air of decrepitude about her. In one hand, she has a mugful of water frothy with soap, that brims over with her every gentle step, and in the other hand, she is clutching a plastic doll. She dunks her doll in the froth and is soon engrossed in rubbing and cleaning it.

Leaving his lines, Basar Mal switches to drawing the seated Mangan's Ma, head bent, washing the little plastic doll. With decisive strokes, he first makes the back of the chair. Then Mangan's Ma's back propped against it. Then makes the seat of the chair. Then Mangan's Ma's salwar-clad seat sticking to it. Then her feet jutting out of the salwar.

A simple shape emerges. By the salwar, one would know it is Mangan's Ma. He doesn't want to add on to it. 'Once the essence of what you're making and what you imagined to convey is clear in the picture, you shouldn't make it any further,' he had tried to explain to Mangan's Ma, a great many years ago.

He doesn't remember what Mangan's Ma had said in response then.

He tells it again. Bending over the mug, wet doll in hand, she looks at him—as though she didn't hear him. He repeats his words. Mangan's Ma's face is still the same, as though she desired to hear the words once more like before. Before, like some moments before. Before, like many years before.

She gets up slowly, collects her things and leaves. From inside comes the sound of water plashing in the wash basin. She has now rinsed her doll with clear water.

Basar Mal thumbs through the pages of his drawing book. Mangan's Ma is missing in the past several pages. He had, after many days, slid his pencil on the contours of her body. Softly he slides his finger once again along it. He cannot remember the last time his fingers had slid on Mangan's Ma's warm flesh. Tenderly, beside the picture, he writes in Sindhi—'Jalo'. Erases it. Then writes in English—'She'. Erases it. Then writes in English again—'Melancholy'.

And the sweet scent of guava fills the room.

So fine is the scent that often a nose cannot discern it. But Basar Mal can recognize this fragrance, he can sense it from afar.

He goes back to an older page. A girl walking away with her back to him, a long plait dangling. On another page, a mango tree.

The mango sapling he planted in a forest just outside the city twenty years ago is now a full-grown, thick-trunked fruit-laden tree. Little does he care how long he lives. But will the tree live? The land mafia is grabbing every inch of Mumbai. The city has been upturned. Will the forest be dug up? His tree uprooted? The nearby forest, like him, will be devoured by hungry sharks.

He shakes his head. No one is immortal. Life goes on, mainly because of the travails required to live. His travails included writing unanswered letters to the Prime Minister, religiously every month, about the bloody land politics and the threatening phone calls.

What would he do if the mafia killed him and buried him under this very land? He tries to think. He would very slowly furrow a tunnel deep underground, inching along in the mud and reach Larkana, then slowly descend upon the place where he had once buried his love letter in a small wooden box, and unbury his love.

He smiles; memories alone are saving him from his nemesis. He lives out the days, remembering and commemorating the past. Remembering is keeping alive a memory. Remembering is love.

The world is saved by love. It is also saved by the memory of love.

He turns the page. A smudged pencil sketch of a child's legs and a football. Scrawled in the corner:

He was destined to come long ago
She is still waiting, even today—

He feels the tiny legs with his hand, then draws two more pairs of legs on either side, one pair clad in pyjamas, the other in salwar. The family is complete.

Mangan's Ma flip-flops into the room, this time dragging a long hosepipe with her. A yellow-coloured rubber pipe that would be about forty feet in length. She has connected one end to the wash basin tap, and she's pulling out its other end. Now she'll wash the street in front of the house.

'Well, well, and why should you wash the road? The entire public goes on it as it is.'

And again, Mangan's Ma looks at Basar Mal, her waist bent by the weight, her head turned towards him, as though she wanted to hear one more time what she just heard—or not heard—as though she wanted to hear something beyond this. Then she moves, dragging her pipe along, and goes out into the street.

He goes to another page. There is a sketch of a lone window inletted into a huge wall of blank sheet. It has only one shutter—the other shutter probably wasn't built or had fallen off somewhere. It has a lattice of big flowers.

He looks at his incomplete sketch. But this is art. What about life? Does it honour incompleteness? A deity is an artwork. And God? We make our own God. *The God of every era looks more incomplete, more imperfect than that of the previous era.* He starts filling the remaining white space in the lattice with crisscrossed lines. After some time, he pauses at another page. An empty bookrack. The books lie scattered on the floor.

He touches the books, an old, lonely man with passionate convictions, his pencil moving with agonizing deliberation on the paper, in a kind of dying away leisureliness:

One dot—is a full stop.
Three dots, dot dot dot—
Things haven't come to an end
Life is on . . .

Next to the books, he draws a gunnysack. Next to it, one more gunnysack. Then one more. Then a plough. Then some bricks. Bricks don't look like bricks. He erases them. Then he erases the gunnysacks. Then the plough. Then the rack. Then the books. He erases everything. He blanks out the whole page.

He fetches a new eraser from the table drawer and gets busy blanking out the whole drawing book.

He cannot remember when he acquired this penchant for drawing and erasing. His drawing book is a palimpsest of a wandering mind. He takes a fresh drawing book, for a while, draws pictures in it, and after a while, erases everything. Then on the same pages, he makes something else until the pages are no longer drawing-worthy.

He wants to become a pencil, so as to add some essential lines to the shape of this world.

He wants to become an eraser, so as to rub off some useless lines from the shape of this world.

Or a window. Or a ball. Or a child. Or a woman. He wants to become everything else other than Basar Mal himself.

He goes out and sits next to Mangan's Ma. She is spraying the street with a jet of water. On her freshly washed road, a motorcycle vrooms and swishes by. Mangan's Ma mutters under her breath. She feels bad about her hard work going to waste.

'They phoned again,' Basar Mal begins, 'The same old things. But I don't want to sell.'

This time Mangan's Ma does not look at him.

He takes the hose from her hand and, sitting next to her, starts washing the street.

'Shall I tell you something, Jalo?' he says, 'Most people in this world want to snatch other people's land. It's not as if they don't have enough, no, it's simply because they have unbridled lust to possess, to conquer. It's not hunger but lust, Jalo! Hunger is sated for a while, but lust isn't, even for a moment. It increases with every fulfilment. Alexander had land, plenty of it, still, he lusted after possessing all the land of this world. He fought many wars, causing millions of deaths. If you see it in today's context, Alexander was not an emperor but the land mafia, who annexed land in every possible way! Every king invading other kingdoms was actually the land mafia. From Napoleon to Hitler to Stalin to Franco. So is every country that encroaches along their shared border, wanting to steal the territory of the neighbouring country. Israel and Palestine and once upon a time, the Soviet Union and now, China swallowing up the land of Tibet. Jinnah wanted land for his people, for himself. He occupied our land. And so, I had to abandon my own soil and sit here. We've historically been victims of different types of land mafia! Today, the mafia is again after me. Can anyone save me from being victimized? Maybe this is my historical fate. Maybe.'

He looks at Mangan's Ma. She is making a circle with her index finger in the pool of water collected near her feet. Again and again she draws the same circle, which silently disappears as soon as it is formed.

He questions himself, 'Who will save you now, Basar Mal?'

'Books!'

Quietly he says to himself.

12

MY NAME IS 'I'

'I went up to the hilltop where there was a temple of the Goddess, but instead of an idol, a mere stone was present. On a tree in front, flags fluttered in the breeze.'
—Nirmal Verma, *A Tune Arising from the Mist*

What I do not understand is why the old man also comes and stands behind me when I stand at the window of the library? Even now, I can sense his rather irksome presence keenly peering out from behind.

I've been coming here for many days now. Almost every evening. The old man has begun to wait for me, which I can sense from his conversations. The first day, he had not even so much as glanced at me. On the second day, he sat cleaning the books. I, too, joined in sprucing them up. How many books there were, and among them, how many

had perished forever! Eaten by termites. Rotting from the
water that dripped from above. Reeking of dust and disuse.
Some even had ants. Together, we worked for two days to
get the books back to their proper shape—dusting, scraping
mildew, gluing pages, and book covers—and then return
them to their racks.

Separating out the damaged books I said, 'Here, these
need to be given to the ragman.'

'Alright, keep them all together at the back.' Those
books never budged from the back.

After that, I shifted the racks from their places.
Rearranged them in such a way that the water dripping
from the roof did not fall straight on them. For many days,
we stayed until eight in the evening instead of leaving at
seven as usual.

And while leaving, I would slip a book or two under
my shirt when the old man was not looking. With honest
intent to read. I was entitled to at least the minimum wage!
I cannot recollect whether it was the fourth, fifth, or sixth
day, but when we were leaving and I had taken the padlock
from the old man's hands to put it on the door, he said, 'At
this rate, the library will become empty, son!' and started
grinning. I felt as if he had put his hand under my shirt,
pulled my pants down, and stripped me naked. Outwardly,
I pretended to pay no heed to what he said, and bowed my
head, busying myself with the lock. Even after snapping it
shut, I kept pulling at it, assuring, reassuring myself. When
I finally lifted my head, I saw the old man clacking his way
out. A stooped figure supported on a stick. A cloth bag

slung from the shoulder. Sparse wispy hair strewn on the collar of his khadi shirt waving from side to side in tandem with his oscillating neck. The library was set down from the walkway. The walkway was a ten-foot ascent. The old man was negotiating it, leaning heavily on his stick.

As if in a trance, I kept watching him. It was purely accidental that the key had remained with me, and for the next two days, I did not go to that street at all.

I had not an inkling that back home, the old man was getting anxious. Two days later when I returned, I found him reading. Despite the soda-bottle glasses he wore, he had to hold a magnifying glass in his hand in order to read. He looked like an archaeologist, sitting in some alleyway of history, attempting to discover words, events, statements, mysteries, and chronicled sorrows by enlarging their images.

I posted myself in front of his table, but he became aware of my presence only when I said, a little sheepishly, '*Whaat Uncle?*'

He looked up. For the first time, I felt how much one could rejoice on seeing someone! With his mouth open, the old man beheld me. He did not utter a single word, but behind his glasses his eyes sparkled in such a way, with his lips spread out in a blissful smile, his wrinkles hanging from cheeks fluttered God knows how many times, and his eyebrows raised in such utter pleasure that I simply stared back! And then the fact that my eyes had lingered on him so long embarrassed me. I was unable to bear his extreme, abundant joy.

This had come unbidden. But I began to realize that the old man now waited for me and that he looked forward to my visits.

But I don't like his following me to the window every time. Whenever I find the girl standing at the yellow window, I, too, prop myself at this end. And he tags along. I can never watch the girl without becoming conscious of the old man breathing down my neck. I have often tried to talk to her using signs and gestures, and I'm sure she would have responded—for she often looks in my direction—but for the old man who keeps standing by my side. I try my best to shoo him away but he does not budge. He comes here on the pretext of giving me coffee, then stands there himself, sipping his own cup. I have come to a firm conclusion, that he is a sly, evil, rotten, dirty old man!

Today, as always, the girl retreats after standing there behind the yellow mesh. I become really angry and glower at the old man, but he still peers out, unaware.

I get up, stride outside, and light a cigarette. The old man straggles after me, dragging a chair along.

'Leave it, Uncle. I'm coming in.'

'Let's sit here for a while . . .'

He places the chair for me to sit. Then he trudges inside to fetch a second chair. I stop him and fetch the second chair myself.

He sits with me, and after a moment's silence says, 'Give me a drag.'

I extend him my cigarette. From here too, the window is clearly visible, but the angle of the view has altered a little.

A shrub hinders the direct view, and I have to crane my neck sideways to see the window clearly.

The old man removes his glasses, keeps them in the pocket, and props his head against the library wall, knotting his hands behind the head.

I see gravel-ballast dumps everywhere. On one side, there is a mound of sand. And on the other side heaped bricks. Cement gunny bags, stacked iron rods. The ground is soft, with sand strewn all over. During the day, perhaps the children frolic and roll on the sand.

'Uncle, why are there so many things lying around? Planning to take up some construction work?' I ask, grinning.

'No, this belongs to the front people. For their renovation.'

'By front people, you mean the folks with the yellow window?'

'Yes.'

Someone extends a hand and pulls the curtain across on the window with yellow shutters and yellow grille. Behind the curtained window, against the light, a shadow flits across every so often.

His eyes follow the path to the window.

'Can you smell the aroma of guava from here?' he asks suddenly.

'No, not at all. Here there's no aroma. None at all.' I try sniffing the air.

'You have not paid attention. It comes. The aroma of guava comes from that window. That's why I like that window so very much . . .'

Hearing this, I burst out laughing. It's like a thunderclap. All my irritation and anger evaporate in the face of this unexpected revelation and after many days I am able to laugh heartily. The old man is embarrassed. His head sinks into his chest and dangles. The old man's face brings me more laughter! Ha Ha Ha! I laugh like a madman. Unashamedly. Even while laughing, I shout out, '*And I, that Window Girl!*'

And laugh louder still.

The old man fumbles for some pebbles in the dark and starts tossing them one by one. There's no sound as they strike the ground. The sound of my laughter slowly begins to fade.

13

THE BOOK COVER TELLS A TALE

'A dream is a scripture, and many scriptures are nothing but dreams.'

—Umberto Eco, *The Name of the Rose*

That boy moved his hand on me, feeling my vellum. I delighted in his touch. There's an expression in English: feeling loved. I felt exactly that—the world's most blissed-out sensation.

I am a book. Touch me. Kiss me. Read me. From start to finish. I am the beginning. I am the end. You don't need to try very hard. If you've felt me with your fingers, then you've kissed me with your eyes. And, if you've pressed your lips against my skin, then you've reposed me in your heart. A sincere touch or a heartfelt kiss is enough to open me up.

I am the oldest book here. I've never been touched. There is only Basar Mal who sometimes brushes the dust off me. I've been screaming, waiting to be touched ever since I was neatly shelved on the rack. No, I haven't wearied of waiting. Honestly, how can I ever weary of it? I've spent my whole life swinging in the cradle of an interminable wait. After all, I am Basar Mal's child, his daughter. That person's daughter who, propping his elbow on a table in a desolate library, has been waiting with a kind of unbreakable conviction for the past many years—that someone will come and borrow a book from his library to read.

Books are the scented consciousness of his wait.

The fiction of wait in this world has been written either by women or by forgotten books like me.

Therefore, when that boy held me, I reveled in that touch. He went about gluing me to my book, he turned me over in his mind, and I had sensed then that he would read me. And lo, he soon set about reading me.

'*I was read*' in the void-mirror reflects as '*I was loved*', the reflection of the inner reflection.

I was happy. I was smiling. The same evening, after Basar Mal and that boy left, and no human soul was present in the library, I danced. Danced a great deal. After many days, in the dead of night, there was a happy dance by books in the library. You see, we often dance here, but usually, our dance is a dance of mourning.

A faint light streamed in from the window. A little moonlight. A little streetlight. Both mingled together and the lambent glow falling across the room reflected the window's elongated square onto the floor, streaked with shadows of shutters and bars. I climbed down from my place and called out loud in the language of books. My call as if roused all other books. Among us was a well-thumbed book, probably the most perused in years gone by. She rose very slowly and teetered towards the windowsill. We still remember how at one time, she used to sing beautifully. She's deferred her singing for a long while now. She sat looking out the window. Then began to sing in a faint, atavistic voice. It was a song about the eternal memory of love. All our faces lit up.

Another book climbed down and placed herself in the middle of a lit square on the floor. We found that the light had transfigured her into a gleaming violin. Bowing, plucking, arco, pizzicato, she glissaded through, rich and mellifluous.

One more book came down. Rolling across, it turned into a dholak. Yet another began trilling flute notes. One became a drum. One, a saxophone.

Chinks shone in the mud tiles in one part of the roof. The rainwater would drip in, slopping over the edge of the chinks. The book straight down often remained soggy. It squelched down and lay on the floor, stretching herself stiff and tall. We saw that she was transfigured into a jal tarang. She tinkled and twirled as if an exhilarated ripple purled.

That night, the library was not a library but a stage. There is music hiding in every book. That night, the music emerged from the pages to sway in the open. Like musical stars scattered across the sky, we twinkled. We sang as one. We caught each other's hands. We stepped together. Our bodies were light and lissome. We were a pullulating inn of flowing tunes. We danced, blithe, in unison.

A book of poetry danced, hugging a book of prose. When a flabby novel while dancing gasped for breath, the other books lovingly carried it and danced. The thin books that would blow away even with a gentle breeze held hands and, forming a line like tribal girls, danced a chorus. Some books, considered awfully boring, and filled with numbers, figures, statistics but not one simple, chaste sentence, danced deliriously like drunken elephants and while dancing, they collided with the lean books. But in that heat of dance, none felt bad about anything.

This was a dance of ecstasy. This was the Great Illusionist Parvati's lasya. In Hindu mythology, when Lord Shiva dances the cosmic dance tandava, then as complement and contrast, his wife Parvati dances lasya.

Tandava, vigourous and virile, can have expressions of *raudra*—the violent rage. Whereas lasya is always a dance of joy. Very delicate, natural, filled with love. The sweet succulence of lasya assuages the fiery aggression of the tandava. We are books. We do not know whose shadow of violent rage is upon us. But at present, we desire to tame all the ferocious *raudra* scourging our lives with this lasya, this joy, this vitality of illusion. Over there, in some invisible Himalayas of the Creation, the daughter of the mountain, Parvati, dances with her Shiva to the beats of hope. Over here, inside an almost ruinous library, we, the daughters of Basar Mal, dance, waiting for our Shiva.

Dance is a hope. Dance is also a wait.

Right opposite the rack where I am stacked is this window where the boy stands. Through the window, a yellow window can be seen in the distance, where oftentimes a girl stands—like she was some long-forgotten book come from somewhere, waiting for someone. I can clearly see the girl's face from here. I can see everything with crystalline sharpness. That night I had a strong urge to bring the girl over and include her in my dance. Wrapping my fine vellum around her waist, waltz. I wanted to tell her:

Touch a book, touch someone with great love. A dance will be born into you.

If the ocean broke into dance inside the earth, wouldn't also the earth appear to be dancing? In much the same way, it is not the dance of the body but love.

Like the elongated shadows falling in the evening sun, when even a small thing, bathed in light, makes a shadow many times more than the actual, the light within builds a humongous shadow of the inexpressible presence in our heart. This is the greater vision of love, of bliss, which, more than the explicit expressibles in our life, is immanent in the inexpressible presences inside our heart.

I wanted to tell her:

What you call dance lives inside your body as an inexpressible love, ardour, compassion. The body dances— and love makes it dance.

Or maybe I am not a book cover, I am that girl of the yellow window?

And maybe my dance is not just the dance of a book, but the dance that spurted inside the heart of that girl?

14

DIL KHUSH

'Should I have to portray a convict—or a criminal—I shall so bedeck him with flowers that, as he disappears beneath them, he will himself become a flower, a gigantic and new one.'
—Jean Genet, *The Thief's Journal*

I see a crowd, and my heart skips a beat!

'What's happening here?'

I toss this stock question to someone standing at the back. He hands an equally stock answer, he ignores my question. Standing on my toes, I try to look over the crowd but fail to see anything. There's only the sound of thwack-thwack, tempered with abuses.

Excuse me . . . Excuse me . . . I start cleaving through the crowd. There is an electric pole adjacent to Dil Khush's shop. Usually, he has his back to it while managing the busy shop. Jutting out of the shop is his big cashbox, and jutting out even further, the other promontories: his kettle, the big gas stove, and a showcase-like glass thing in which his samosa, vada, bhajia are shoved.

I see a boy, about seventeen years old, tied to the electric pole. The boy has been trussed up with his shirt. Only his trousers are on him. A man swears and punches him hard. The boy squirms in pain. His eyes are half-closed, and the lids swollen. His lips dribble spittle. Every time his head hangs down, the man grabbing his hair yanks it up and jabs him on the jaw. Then, another man joins him, wielding a stick.

'Kill him!' he spits in anger.

'Kill him!' the place reverberates.

The man now beats the poor boy's legs with the stick.

The sound of thwack-thwack mixing with the uproarious glee of the crowd is sowing panic. Dil Khush is also standing nearby. In the midst of his big head and beard, where I always saw his shining teeth, I spot dread. 'Stop!' he cries. 'You will kill the boy! Please stop it . . .' his voice breaks, appealing to the men. He begs them to let go of the boy. His hands shake. Perhaps his legs, too. I know he suffers from high blood pressure. When he sees me, he comes to stand by my side. When I ask him the matter, he clasps my hand tight and shaking his head says, 'No idea, but they say the boy stole. They were marching him down to the police station when, I don't know why, right in front of my shop, they started this drama.'

A man in the crowd busily takes pictures of the boy being pummeled against the backdrop of Dil Khush's shop on his handycam. Some others click on their cell phone cameras. I had, not long ago, watched on TV, a boy knocked down to death at the gates of a Chennai college, an autorickshaw fellow in Delhi struck down, and a woman in Meerut beaten up in similar frenzied street scenes.

This handycam-wielding man will, in the name of citizen journalism, sell this video to some TV channel. The TV channel will then twist it, sensationalize it, perhaps communalize it, and the whole nation will watch it as 'breaking news' at dinnertime.

For the first time, I see a boy look like a nation. Like my own nation. Being beaten up by some and watched by many.

I join Dil Khush in protesting noisily. '*Stop it, man!*' I shout, 'You will kill him.' Then I begin screaming wildly, 'Untie the boy! Someone untie him! Let's go to the police.' Now Dil Khush joins me in screaming. His servant, too. 'Let's go to the police,' the tensed place resonates.

Whether it was the effect of our screaming, or the exhaustion of beating, or the entry of two constables ripping through the crowd, the men stop beating the boy. They drag a bench from Dil Khush's shop and slump on it, panting heavily. The hapless boy lies motionless. He is probably dead. In the din of fading sounds, people start leaving. The place becomes quiet. The men glare into Dil Khush's face, hate brimming their eyes. They spit on the ground. Dil Khush gulps involuntarily.

'Let's go inside,' I tell Dil khush and start hurrying towards the seclusion of the shop, pulling him along. But he stops me with a shake of his head. He stands there atremble with fear. His voice sounds so shaky that it seems he will start bawling any moment.

A sick feeling washes over me as I look at the boy. I feel something strange in my chest. A thick thread of spittle dribbling from his mouth dangles to his knees. Swinging softly. The thread slowly stretches long until it touches the ground. Then it snaps. Part of it rebounds and sticks back to the mouth.

Dil Khush's servant, with servile timidity, gives water to the two men who beat up the boy, and also to the two constables. The constables sit with them on the bench. They question, and the beaters answer—designating their brutality with metaphors oozing the fragility of a flower.

One of the beaters throws the leftover water from his glass on the boy's face. The boy's head makes an almost imperceptible, yet distinct movement.

15

MY NAME IS 'I'

> 'Nineties marketers have dutifully come up with clever and intrusive
> new selling techniques. Gordon's gin experimented with filling
> British movie theatres with the scent of juniper berries; Calvin
> Klein stuck 'CK Be' perfume strips on the backs of Ticketmaster
> concert envelopes . . .'
>
> —Naomi Klein, *No Logo*

For the past three or four months, I've had abundant idle
time on my hands, and he is after my life. That's why I run
away from my Pau, literally.

After spending a few hours on the net in the morning,
I loaf outside. I consider net surfing my time for struggle.
During this time, I send my resumé to headhunters or
upload it to various job sites. If I know that the knowledge
of something would someday serve me, I make every effort

to learn it. From corporate history to the history of books, music, and art. I also strive to improve my English, having deferred it for too long. In short, my time in the morning is for job hunting and equipping myself better for the design I have in mind.

But I am secretive about my plans and don't disclose anything to my Pau. My reticence makes my father upset. Soon after the exam results, many of my friends lost no time in hitching themselves to various jobs, while I still sit around, with my self-assured bearing, ostensibly doing nothing—that I appear useless to my father. But I know, whoever has found a job, here and there, is sticking it out for a paltry two to three lakh rupees, with plans to switch after six months. I don't have the time or the patience to make an austere compromise with my ideals. A petty pay package of two–three lakhs is so below me that I haven't even deigned to consider it. I have the guts to reject such offers and also the confidence that I'll get what I want through some merciless bargaining.

But not everything is by design, I suppose. Constantly tending to books, I have unwittingly begun reading them, although I never slipped a book under my shirt after that incident.

I remember the first book I read was Marquez's *No one Writes to the Colonel*. I've begun to like biographies and autobiographies, many times reading them in Marathi. Bunuel's *My Last Sigh*; Ingrid Bergman's autobiography; Mary Pickford, Douglas Fairbanks, Vivian Leigh, and Clark Gable's biographies. And Allan Sealy's splendid *The Everest*

Hotel. In all these books, the old man would be present, sometimes hesitant, sometimes loud and clear, with his scrawny signature and pencil markings. Like some faded dust-coloured tailed star, his pencil would have passed by the saddest lines, perhaps underlining their sorrow and pain. The pages that make eyes cry, their corners would be dog-eared—they had probably been read and re-read several times. There would be scrawled notes, forgotten and silent, pressed between pages.

I fail to fathom the strange relationship of my own mind to the books, and the strange bond these books made between me and the old man.

That night, having finished Ingmar Bergman's *The Magic Lantern*, I open the dissertation on 'Marlboro Friday Crisis' on my computer, but before I can begin reading it, my father blusters into the room. I wonder, is it the dissonant wind from the open window or something in the heat that I sense disapproval? Can't I exist without having to explain myself? But to ward off an impending argument, I think it wise to show him the email with the four-lakh-rupee job offer.

'I am negotiating for at least one and half more, Pau,' I tell him, 'But even if they offer me an increase of one lakh, I am ready to join.' (It would still be more than what my Pau gets presently.)

Instead of being pleased, my implacable Pau loses his temper. 'If you can't even join for four, then God be your saviour!' he tells me, that same dissonance in his voice, 'Don't be greedy, boy. Go slow.'

'Pau, when people can get a start offer of ten lakhs, shouldn't I even have a five-lakh start?' I ask.

'You need experience!' he says, with outraged concern, 'We get three and a half, but only after long years of work. After building trust in the company.'

'Arré Pau, stop it now!' I say sharply, 'You aren't market aware. You should be daring and not bowing when you ask for a job. You people bowed and worked, that's why remained tamed. You speak of old security and experience. But there's no such thing. Ten of your age will be under me where I join, and all year round they'll bow to me, so that I recommend a good increment for them.'

A chastened Pau does not say anything. He sits down and picks up *The Magic Lantern*. I think he will now sit a long time here. I sneak back into my 'Marlboro Friday'.

My father sits silently, absently flipping the pages, and I know I have hurt him. 'Please, Pau,' I say in a milder, gentler tone, 'Try to understand. I know how to plan my career. I am not praising myself, but if I'm sitting idle so confidently, then I probably have something in my hands. Please drop your "unemployment" complex.'

'I believe in branding,' I try to explain. 'Brands conjure an image. If at the beginning itself, my brand gets linked with some mediocre company, I'll only have problems going ahead. You know how badly I want to start big. And I will. Because I have passion and knowledge. Experience will come anyway, by and by. Don't hold me in such contempt as to take me for an underdog—and please stop talking like an old goof, my young Pau!' I moan desperately.

In my tone, there is pleading now, the way one pleads when one is helpless. Despite everything, I was his flesh and blood. I loved him dearly, and I wanted him to see it.

But God's motives are otherwise. He makes sure that despite my good intentions, I should be misunderstood. This happens in almost all my relationships.

I start playing with the table lamp switch, making the lamp blink on and off. The wind is loud in the window. My Pau motions to me, with a gesture of his hand, to stop twiddling with the switch.

'So you feel I should stop speaking?'

What answer could one possibly give to such a typical melodramatic question?

Right after it, he'll start picking on me. He'll disapprove of my smoking, my habit of walking, having an occasional beer, and going out with girls. Then he'll say I am distracted, dreamy, and overconfident. That such was not the case in their times. That he built this house after twenty years of working. Now, how can I tell him that two years in a job and one can build a bigger house? That his attitude makes Ma suffer? That a smoke, a beer, and a walk are my ways of focusing, energizing, and working out? That I am so into this plan of mine that I don't care about the girls I roam with? But I know, in spite of my explanations even a million times, he will play his sarcastic tape:

'You have all the passion and knowledge, boy! I'm just an old goof. What can I say?'

'Oh no! Again that clichéd generation gap funda. Pau, just let me be . . .'

But my Pau had risen and left. He suddenly got up after speaking, his eyes teared, and his lips trembled. His legs probably shook while leaving. My poor Pau, again, he is hurt unnecessarily.

'Shit! To hell with Pau! To hell with all this!'

:(

There are times when my father wants to show his love to me, and I laugh in derision. And there are times when I want to show my love to him, and he retracts, feeling hurt. It seems to me that a closed cave exists between me and my father: neither of us knows how to open this cave, and reach across to the other side. The magical Simsim floats without our knowledge somewhere in an obscure space of our lives.

I lean back in my chair and shut my eyes.

Where together should be, is opposite.
Where for you should be, is against you.
Where healing should be, is suppurate.

The night wind is the roughest wind. It opens frail bindings.

The Magic Lantern sighs.

From the flows of wind and flapping pages comes a rhythmic lull that brings comfort just like that mother who, with her weight of poverty, old clothes and cooking pots, lulled me in her womb as she struggled between nine long platforms to find the right train, dumbstruck by the sounds of an alien language and an alien city, meeting words, curses, swears with her thin brave silence.

The space my Pau left empties into me.

16

THE OLD MAN'S STORY

'When we came to settle here we did not know about the ants. We'd be all right here, it seemed that day; the sky and green looked bright, too bright, perhaps, for the worries we had, my wife and I—how could we have guessed about the ants?'
—Italo Calvino, *The Argentine Ant*

Basar Mal is lost between the two open doors of the wooden closet. Whenever he opens this closet, he feels a world has opened before him. A world completely unknown to him. A biggish globe, soft and squashy. Wherever he touches it, the finger sinks in. To extricate his finger, he presses the globe with his hand, and the hand gets stuck. In an attempt to remove this hand, the other hand, too, gets mired down. This mire chases him constantly, trapping him into the hidden worlds that lie beneath every spot he touches.

He takes out a plastic carry bag and quickly closes the door. Oh, the oddments inside the closet! Clothes hanging on the rail. Are they clothes? They are humans. Files lying in the locker. Are they files? They are, in truth, all of history. All of life itself is history. Peep in, and you'll get caught. Blessed forgetfulness comes with practice. Indeed, at his age, everything appears to be merely a chapter of memory.

Once again, he opens the closet door. He always has an odd feeling of a presence inside this closet, ignored and left out. Even after talking to every occupant, he hesitates—there is something in this silent closet that never gets touched. That he hasn't been able to talk to, yet.

His tobacco pipe lies invitingly in front of him.

There used to be a shop in Flora Fountain opposite Akbarallys, and Mangan's Ma, that is, his wife Jalo, had got him the pipe from there. A calabash pipe with a meerschaum bowl. It looked like a miniature saxophone to him. Along with it, she'd bought some Van Gogh tobacco as well. For days, Basar Mal would hold the pipe in his mouth and only at night, before going to bed, remove it. Once in a while, he would fill tobacco in the pipe and have a smoke.

An old packet of Van Gogh still lies next to the pipe, probably gone bad by now. He sniffs it. It smells exactly like the aroma that rose, at one time, out of Jalo's armpits, right after her bath. A mix of body, sweat, soap, and powder. He turns around and sees Jalo sound asleep on the bed. A wooden harmonica lies beside her. She had bought it from a street fair for Mangan a long time ago.

Basar Mal smiles, pleased that he remembers everything. He once again inhales his Van Gogh. 'I am a connoisseur of fragrances,' he says with a chuckle. Holding the pouch in his hand, he goes to Mangan's Ma, his Jalo. Her lips are tightly pursed, as if they had never been there. Deep lines from the chin run upwards to her lower lip. Cheeks are scooped out. They are two hollows now, as if struck by the meteors of time.

Tenderly, he presses his lips in the hollow space. It feels as if his lips have sunk in deep somewhere. Gliding them, he tries to see if he can feel the wrinkles on the cheeks? He can only feel the touch of cool and doughy skin. The breath travels from his nose, touches her cheek, and returns to the space between his nose and upper lip. He closes his eyes and, very slowly, lets his lips brush against her cheek. It feels like his lips are moving on small white stones, smoothened by the gusty waves of a river. One more warm breath.

Jalo does not stir. The sinews in his calves start to feel the stretch, having stood bent over for so long, holding her face in his palms. He moves away and drags a chair to sit on. Jalo had especially got this wooden chair made for them. It was similar to the one in Van Gogh's 'Bedroom in Arles'. Basar Mal had shown her the artwork when he saw the tobacco she'd got him. She had liked this painting in particular because, in it, there was a room similar to what she called the room of pain. She would say, 'Someone emerges from this room, and at the same moment, someone else is about to enter it. It is an in-between state—of an empty room, with one *at* one door going out, and another *at* another door expected in.

The state we are in, our whole life, one day after another, interminably, in the expectation of living.'

He fills his meerschaum with the vintage Van Gogh tobacco and gets a matchbox from the kitchen. He has lost practice lighting a pipe. He takes a deep draw and throws the smoke up. There is very little smoke. The tobacco does not achieve a good burn. He puts the plastic carry bag on the table and the Van Gogh chair back in its place.

Jalo is in a deep sleep. On her ancient cheeks, he catches sight of a window.

Peeping out of the madrasa window, that girl Jaam had made all sorts of demands. Once, she was obstinate about riding on a bicycle with him.

'Give me a ride on your cycle,' she said, more than sixty years ago.

Basar Mal hesitated.

'But you have a motorcar in your house. Why do you want to sit on a cycle?'

'It will be like sitting on your lap,' Jaam said with an impish smile.

'If someone sees us, then?'

'That's your problem. I want to ride with you on your cycle, and that's that.'

The bicycle belonged to Basar Mal's father. He used it to go to his shop or the bank and didn't let Basar Mal use the cycle without asking at least ten questions. And never in the afternoons.

But Basar Mal had promised to meet her in the afternoon.

The day suddenly comes back sharp and alive, as though his mind's papers have been dusted and the writing is now legible.

That afternoon, he hid behind the tree in front of their shop, waiting for an opportunity. He could see his father sitting on a cotton mattress on the floor and working. As soon as his father went into the inner room, Basar Mal, avoiding the servants, swiftly opened the lock of the bicycle parked on the street and vamoosed. He was sweating out of fear as he rode to the madrasa, but didn't stop until he reached it.

Perhaps God had saved the deserted and desolate madrasa from the eyes of the world for these two. Carrying the cycle on his shoulders, he climbed up the steps of the madrasa, and sat in the compound to wait for Jaam. She came after a good half hour. He made Jaam sit on his bicycle and went in circles inside the compound along its wall.

'O Cycle Man, take me to Lahore,' she said.

'Madam Ji, this will go only up to Shahdadkot. To Lahore, it will be double fare,' Basar Mal said, in a patronizing way.

'Double?' Jaam laughed. In her laughter resonated the most sacred sound of this world. The same laughter that, after six decades, he hears, sometimes from inside the thermos, sometimes from the book almirah.

They both got dizzy from going round and round. Dropping the cycle, they lay down on the compound grass. Basar Mal was breathless, she was all smiles, while the yellow window looked quietly down at them from the tall madrasa wall.

By the time Basar Mal reached the shop in the evening, his father, thinking the bicycle was stolen, had caused considerable commotion. When he saw the cycle safely back, he first heaved a sigh of relief, then didn't look right, didn't look left, and gave Basar Mal a dressing-down. The next three days, he kept asking his son, sometimes in a loud voice, sometimes lovingly: 'Where did you go with my cycle, Basar Mal?'

And every time, in response Basar Mal gave a big, stupid smile. As though someone had hypnotized him.

He feels as if he is still holding the handle with both hands, and in between his arms, the fairy-like Jaam is still sitting on his bicycle. And time has frozen still.

Didn't that madrasa window, with its yellow shutters and lattice of big yellow flowers, look the same as the Mool Chandani's opposite the library? Perhaps, the window broken down with a rioter's axe more than half a century ago had travelled from Larkana all the way here to dwell in this wall opposite the library?

'If the window has wandered for so many years, maybe it has been searching for me, waiting for me.'

He opens the carry bag and takes out a file. Basar Mal, who remembers everything, cannot remember when he had last opened this file to look into it.

When would Jaam open her veil to look at him?—Basar Mal always remained in that wait. His memory has archived the last glimpsed image of her: holding a dark green guava, biting the rawness with her teeth. That last time she had agreed, after much pouting and sulking, that they would go to Shahdadkot first, and they decided to meet three days later at the madrasa window before sunrise. Her eyes were laughing with the excitement of eloping with him. She had, swiftly turning back, slid away the veil from her face and said, 'If you don't come, I'll think your love is fake. Even that letter which you wrote to me.' He had wanted to say something in return, but she had snorted 'hunh!' and flapped her veil back on. Does he remember that rapidly disappearing figure behind the veil? Does he remember the ringing laughter sifting through the gossamer?

'Well, well, Basar Mal, there's so much you don't remember!'

He strikes a match and lights his pipe.

That same evening, riots had broken out in Larkana. Punjab had erupted already. But he had been heedless in his love. Sindh, like him, lived in delusion that it was immune to riots, justified by strong communal love. Punjab had been partitioned. The Sindhi Hindus hoped that their land would likewise be divided, a portion of which would go to Hindustan, and they would gradually migrate to that part. But Sindh remained whole and in Pakistan. The hopes of the Sindhi Hindus had entangled them in an illusionary belief and a laze-filled indecision. It was all too late. The muhajirs from Hindustan had begun moving directly to Sindh and were settling everywhere, in Karachi, Hyderabad, Larkana, Shikarpur. They intended, and so coerced the Sindhi Muslims, to drive away the Hindus by main force or otherwise.

And Larkana that night ignited.

Suddenly, near the door to the main thought, he stops, trying to recollect what he had witnessed back then, and remembering that he had, at the time, written down the events goes to his books. His hands almost tremble as he searches through books, eventually managing to draw out a sheaf of old papers. Even now, after all these years, as he looks at the smudged graphite, a hurricane sweeps through him. The paper is blurred, written sixty years ago from Delhi's Tughlakabad refugee camp, where he was sheltered for more than a month. It is a long memory of an eighteen-year-old boy which, he now thinks, begins rather poetically:

* * *

My story may seem unbelievable, but believe me, disbelief is the name of the first stairstep into the black well of disappointment.

I was a lover. Someone's beloved. I hadn't got anything to do with politics. The sparks had been kindled many months before. My parents would talk in urgent, low voices, discussing the future. But I was unaware of all such discussions. Not until the night when Larkana ignited did the flames of communal riots lick me.

That midnight, a mob of Muslims came and hurled rocks at Hindu houses, a warning notice for us to clear out. We looked through the windows. We couldn't know who those Muslims were. Were they of our city? Our acquaintances? It was so dark we couldn't see their faces. An emergency meeting of the neighbourhood was called, and the elders decided that we should pack up our belongings and leave, but most did not approve; how could they just throw away a lifetime of earnings and their homes and go to the unfamiliar regions of Hindustan? Sindh was their homeland!

Some young Hindu men of the locality quietly grouped together and went out in the night to pelt angry rocks at the Muslim houses. Everything was surprisingly normal the next day, and we sighed and trembled with relief. But as soon as evening fell, they came. They were probably waiting for the cover of darkness. The strains of *Allah hu Akbar* resonated in the streets. We leaned out of the first-story window. A crowd stood down— masked faces holding naked swords and lit torches waiting for something ominous to happen. A single stone that night from our side was certain to have triggered arson. Thankfully, our youths kept quiet that night.

After a while, a leaderlike person stepped forward from the crowd and shouted in Urdu, 'Alhamdulillah! We do not want any bloodshed; we have come to say that all Hindu brothers and sisters should please pack their belongings and quietly leave. This is our last communication. There will be no more cautioning. After the evening of tomorrow, we'll be silent, and our torches and swords will speak.'

In our Sindh, no Hindu or Muslim spoke Urdu this refined because it was not our language. That leaderlike person had definitely come from either Delhi or Lucknow. The nobility of style and the delicacy and refinement of the tongue are found in those regions. We lay hiding in the upstairs rooms, fearing him, fearing for our lives and, at the same time, out of curiosity, which once in a while prevailed over our fear, we whispered among ourselves about that person's fine poetic tongue.

Father remarked, 'From the east, an elegant, well-mannered terror has arrived.'

By the next afternoon, we had packed our luggage. Father sat all night lovingly tying our things. He had government bonds worth thousands of rupees. Perhaps they were useless now. Still, he kept them carefully in his briefcase. The rest of the things were packed in iron trunks. Mother had some gold chains and necklaces. She stitched them in the hem of her kurta and salwar. In ordinary-looking clothes, she stitched her small earrings.

Father would repeatedly come to the inner rooms, saying, 'We have absolutely no idea what the journey will be like. I have heard the refugees may have to spend months in camps. I can't guess which city the Hindustan government would send us to. It might take years for us to settle, to find a job. So, take all your valuables, hide them in grains and clothes. Who knows when we'll need them— Jhulelal has to help us cross over all hurdles!'

We were beginning an uncertain and dangerous journey. We were scared, but in us, there was also a hope of crossing over to life.

And all the while, Jaam's voice hung, soft, sonorous above the din of the preparations and parents' instructions, ceaselessly echoing in my mind and body like a dream away from reality. I was ashamed how, like a coward, I was running away with my family to another country instead of running away with her to Shahdadkot.

But I worried and I worried; it seemed like I could never succeed in sneaking her a message. I delved into the possibility of both families leaving Larkana together, but I knew it was a futile thought.

We caught the afternoon bus to Karachi. Whenever we heard *Allah hu Akbar* in the distance, we whispered, 'ya Allah, mercy!' which was strange irony. Our living had blended with theirs so much so that even at the time, 'ya Allah' came out of our mouths and not 'hey Ram.' We couldn't change the language of the tongue even if we wished, but the truth is, we had also become scared of the word 'Allah.' Our fears hide inside our language.

Shortly before midnight, we arrived at the refugee camp in Karachi. It was like a mega jamboree, full of noise and dust. Lights yawned along the overcrowded camp. Groans, cries, frantic despair, and melancholic festivities were as if caught in a timeless present that did not know the meaning of night.

Someone's bagful of money was lost, and he hollered up and down, pleading with the policemen. Someone's baby was lost. The mother sat crying, silent and hopeless, tears streaking her face. An elderly man from Shikarpur lay on the ground, his arm across the chest clutching his heart, while his benumbed family frantically searched for a doctor, eventually finding a nurse. The nurse clarified that all doctors had been sent to the refugee camp on the other side of the field. That camp was for the muhajirs coming from Hindustan. We were Sindh's own people, but Karachi did not worry about us anymore. Their priority was the muhajirs coming from across. An absolute religious precedence that swallowed the basic human priorities. In one stroke, everything changed! Until a few days ago, this place used to be Hindustan. Now it was Pakistan. All resources, comforts and amenities were for those who wanted to remain Pakistani. And for those who did not, the government machinery had begun to treat them like outsiders. I realized, for the first time, that just by a change of name of the country, our fate quietly translates our fortunes into misfortunes.

Before our eyes, the Shikarpur elder died, his hand clutching his chest.

Sitting in the middle of the family guarding the luggage, my harried father said, 'To be a refugee is a monstrous curse. No sooner is the land taken from us than the mountain of troubles falls on our heads. Even Adam wasn't this homeless after being banished from Eden, the way a refugee is after losing their land.'

There were many routes to Hindustan; cheaper options were fraught with danger, the expensive ones safer. I realized one had to be both lucky and moneyed to cross the border safely. In times of crisis, relying on luck is not a choice but a helpless compulsion. We were helpless but not without options.

Father chose the expensive route, of sailing by ship, for he loved us well. It was decided that at daybreak, we would board the ship to Bombay.

I was distraught because I couldn't leave Jaam back there in Larkana and couldn't take her where we were going. I couldn't stitch her in the hem of my pyjamas, or hide her in the grain box, or carry her in a gunny bag. 'But you can hold her hand,' I confronted myself. I had to prove to her and to myself that I wasn't a coward to flee like that, leaving her behind just to escape death.

My family was asleep on newspapers spread on the ground. I quietly slung my bag and headed towards the main gate of the refugee camp. Even as I was crossing the gate, the sensation remained that at any moment, my parents would wake and call out after me, 'Where are you going, Basar Mal?'

But I walked, swift and silent, out the gate and couldn't hear anything.

Leaving my entire family sleeping at the refugee camp in Karachi, I returned to Larkana.

* * *

Basar Mal cannot read any further. He is suddenly cold. A wrinkled shiver rises inside his chest. Like a whirlpool, it wheels round and round and settles somewhere there. He gets up and, taking out a Hyderabadi shawl from the closet, covers Jalo.

The file lies untouched on the table. But he knows what it contains. Legal documents, yellow with age: Barrack Number 918/9, 1700 square feet land, ownership to Basar

Mal Jetharam Purswani on orders of the Indian Government and Bombay Municipality—marked correspondingly on a map is Sindhu Library, the library he had built on this land. On water-proof paper, the carbon copy of the map illustrates the building walls, arrow directions, feet measurement, and markings. Next to the building, a street is marked. And some boxes, that have been coloured with slant lines. But the map provides no space for bookracks. No mention of the wood of the roof, or the pantiles and the water that drips from there. No books on that map. No fragrance from books.

No human appears on any map of the world. A map of humanity never gets made. How, years ago, the map of Hindustan was violently sundered into two pieces, and Basar Mal found no mention of any swarming uprooted multitude on the fragmented map. His nose had, however, picked up a faint reek of the burning pyres.

Basar Mal wants to sprawl out the land papers in front of him. With a thick black marker, erect a tombstone, a slab of stone marking his grave and on it, inscribe this epitaph:

Sindhu Library: Under this land, among silent souls and fallen stars, sleeps Basar Mal Jetharam Purswani, resident of Mumbai, migrant from Larkana, Sindh (Pakistan), along with his books whom he called his daughters. No, he does not sleep but, wide awake, wanders under, among the dust of paper, chanting like a mantra, 'I won't give up my land, I won't give up my land', for eternity, without fear.

The thought brings a smile to his face. The phone calls had become incessant now. Threats sharper. Nastier. He scans the land papers carefully. A tombstone had already been erected and lettered in gothic relief. He could feel it in his bones. Only, it wasn't visible to him until now. Things not visible to the eye, they, too, have an existence, gravid with meaning.

He lights his pipe once again. Rests his head against the back of the chair. Jalo is groaning and turning in her sleep. He looks at her lovingly: *I will come as a heedless smile in your heedless dream.*

He feels the aroma of books around him. He hums to himself, 'If not for fragrances, how would life pass? Thanks to the aromas in my life, I can stand on my own two feet. The aroma of guava, of Van Gogh rising out of armpits, of books springing from inside the bindings.'

Closing the land documents file, he picks up the stick from the table and, blowing smoke, starts pacing up and down the length between the table and bed.

17

MY NAME IS 'I'

'What I didn't know was the truth. In a way, my very presence was a lie.'

—Carlos Fuentes, *The Years with Laura Diaz*

I feel when I'm not with him, he goes about remembering me, and when I'm there right in front of him, his entire wait mutates into a wordless communication of just hmmm and mm-hmm and uh-huh. He remains irresponsive to my presence and my utterances. Sometimes I feel he calls all sorts of jobs to mind only when he sees me. The old man ought to know that I haven't learnt library science, even then, he engages me in organizing his library. Like my Pau, who knows I haven't dabbled in home science, still, there will be an everyday discussion on the practice of good housekeeping. I don't know anything about career counselling, too (nor does my Pau), but still a thousand and one things about a 'decent' career!

It seems people are alike up to a certain age. Then after an intervening gap, from a certain age onward, they become alike again. My Pau and this old man—both alike. The difference would only be in the arithmetic of their ages. All the same, I dare not smoke in front of my Pau, dare not even imagine that he would share my cigarette. With him around, I cannot casually sit at a window to gaze out. In front of Pau and with Pau, a great many things I cannot or dare not do.

* * *

Last night's incident with Pau still rankles. When I reach the library, I find the old man standing by the window. Cupping the stick with both hands. A lone figure—made from his own shadow, melded with it. Filling his heart with the song of his own voice. But I don't like his standing at the window. The old man's presence there meant either some activity behind the curtains of the window across, or that yellow face peeping out. I go and stand behind him.

For the first time, a shutter on the yellow window is closed. Through the open shutter, the curtain shivers mildly. The wall is wet beneath the window, and moss grows there. In some places, the plaster has flaked off. The exposed bricks peep from underneath.

Noticing me behind him, the old man withdraws from the window. Perhaps he doesn't like my standing behind him either. He dodders off to his books. There are some books still on the floor. For the past many days, we've been covering the books with old newspaper. With a thick marker pen, we write the name of the book and its number on the side of the cover. This was essentially my idea. The books would remain safe then, I felt. I don't know why but he agreed to it very reluctantly. But ever since he agreed, he has been at it continuously. I cover the books, then write the name and number on the side. Meanwhile, he sits on a stool beside me thumbing the pages of some book. When I finish and tell him, he writes in a new register the name of the book and the writer, the identification number, and the rack number. Then until I call out again, he goes back to turning the pages of some other time.

But we still found ants, even in the freshly covered books. The old man, in his forgetfulness, would often keep a block of jaggery in the same sling bag in which he kept a book. A little jaggery would stick to the book. When the book came to the rack or the table, ants would get the scent of the jaggery. An ant would nibble at the jaggery. And then, a whole column of ants would be at it.

'There are ants in the book. And this is their study time,' the old man would say of the ants.

I once protested, 'But the ant does not read books. It eats the jaggery sticking to books.' To which he said with a wide grin, 'But jaggery does not stick to all books.'

I draw my chair closer to the window, take out a cigarette from my pocket, and drop an old smallish bowl from the table on my lap as an ashtray. Exhaling the smoke, I slip once again into the same waiting—for the window to open, for her to materialize at any moment and return my love-filled gaze.

The old man suddenly interrupts my lovesick stupor.

'Do you hear the sound of laughter?'

I refocus and try listening to all sounds carefully.

'No,' I tell him.

At least once, every day, he asks me this question and each time I tell him no.

He will also say something like, 'Come here, come here, look at this book (or this room or that window or his sleeve or inside the thermos or the thin mattress on the floor or its bolster), how it smells! Perhaps it is the aroma of the guava.'

I go to him and turn the book this way and that, sniffing everywhere. Umpteen times. Then grimace, 'No Uncle. There's just the stink of fungus.'

He winces, 'Can't you distinguish an aroma from a stink?'

'It is a stink . . . pure unadulterated stink, Uncle!' I answer, keeping a straight face.

'One day this aroma will haunt you.'

For the first time he delivered a solid dialogue, just like in the movies. Pursing my mouth, I fizz out laughing.

'Uncle, this aroma is *haunting* me already. We have to search for this aroma daily, no?' I coddle him with great affection.

He begins to smile. From inside the soda-bottle glasses, his soft, moist eyes are laughing. Small narrow slits. Pitch-black pupils shone in them once. Now the colour of the pupils has faded and turned the colour of dust. A hint of white encircles their outer edges. If one peeped into these, a heavy mist would engulf the heart. Round, thin lips. And small, even teeth. Pendulous cheeks. Some wrinkles. And around the lips, tiny strands of fine grey hair that have escaped the shaving blade.

He withdraws to his chair.

'Does any aroma come from your DVDs?'

I remain impassive. Perhaps he posed this question because I had once compared the DVDs with the books. After a pause, I ask him smilingly, 'Uncle, won't you offer me coffee today?'

Without a glance, he opens the drawer. He takes out a ten-rupee note and a five-rupee coin, 'Go get it. There's no milk today.'

I come back with the milk, and find him inside, struggling with the stove.

'It's not working. You try.'

'In my whole life, I have never lit a stove, Uncle! I don't even know how it works.'

He picks up a rag, wipes the soot off his hands, then takes the milk from my hand. It is ice cold. The thin icicles crusted on the plastic packet are turning soft, slowly melted by the sluggish heat from outside and from our hands, and falling off everywhere.

We come back to the table. With an air of '*leaveit Uncle, lettit go*' about me, I drift back to the window. The lone open shutter of the yellow window is flapping softly.

He opens a register and, calling me over, asks me to connect a call on his cell phone. I do it and then withdraw to my window. After speaking with someone in Sindhi, he waddles over and hands me the cold packet of milk.

'Go along by that window, to the left is a door. The nameplate says Mool Chandani. I have asked them. They'll heat the milk,' he says, pointing at the yellow window.

The prospect of actually meeting the girl I'm so obsessed with in my imagination, who has taken my Imbelo's place, makes me nervous. Really nervous. I protest, 'Arré, Uncle! Leave it. I don't want coffee anymore.'

I hesitate for a long time. Then, finally, I rise to my feet and leave, milk packet in hand, thinking all along, how weird it would look . . .!

I imagine that the door was ajar. A gentle nudge and it would open. Inside, there would be a mysterious darkness and a sweet fragrance, and amidst all this, there she would stand. Before I can imagine any further, the door appears.

I have to ring the calling bell twice before the door yawns open. It is her. No words would tumble out my mouth. She stands there at the door, but I feel as if she is standing at the window. Her lips droop the same way. Perhaps for entire centuries, these lips hadn't smiled. The same half-open eyes, as if for centuries an indolent wakefulness waited for a deep sleep.

She immediately takes the milk packet from my hand and retreats inside. I stand in the middle of the open doorway. In the front is a room, where I can see an old woman lying on the bed, and an old man sitting on the couch with the TV remote in his hand. I inch forward. The TV is on, but without any sound. An old-time comedian is prancing around wearing shorts. On the entire black-and-white screen, only the channel name and the 'mute' symbol supply any colour. The old man is not at all amused by the comedian's antics. He sits straight and taut, like a statue, holding the remote between his thighs with both hands.

All of a sudden, the girl reappears before me.

'It will take at least ten minutes. Come back after ten minutes if you like, or else you can sit inside.' She retreats into the house again.

I come in. On the right, there are the two oldies, and on the left, a door through which I can see the window. I go straight into that room, oblivious to the consequences.

It is a bedroom. Possibly the girl's. The computer is on. Drawing the chair slightly away from the computer, I sit on it in such a way that I can see the TV in the next room, and that old man, and this computer, and if I swing the revolving chair to my right, also this whole room.

On the yellow-shuttered and flower-meshed window, a yellow curtain is drawn. Very little light filters through. The wall above it is awfully damp. Flakes of plaster have chipped off. A framed black-and-white sepia-toned picture, like the ones we find in gift stores, is on the wall.

In the picture, a young man, perhaps English, hung from a train on a deserted platform, and extending his hand held an English girl who stood on the platform. Perhaps the train had started moving and perhaps the girl was left on the platform, and the youth, perhaps climbing in first, wanted to, perhaps, pull her in now. The girl was clutching a bouquet of roses in her other hand: perhaps she had brought it for the boy, or before climbing in, perhaps, the boy had given it to her. Steeped in this perhaps-like uncertain darkness, only the flowers were coloured in that picture.

In the room, I also see a small plastic cooler on which all sorts of almost-used-up thingummies lie idle, including some squeezed-up tubes of face cream. On the computer screen in front of me, the email is open. The draft folder, with a half-written mail. The recipient space is blank. Above, the chat window blinks intermittently.

There is a message in the chat from one 'my name is Joker': wru? :-(

I don't dare look at the computer. The feeling of someone's presence in the room watching me read the messages is palpable. But undeterred by my nervousness, curiosity slides the chat box up——

me (probably this girl): but . . . *main aana nahin chahti.* I don't want to come.

my name is Joker: nopes! u'll hav to :-*

me: GTH :-/

my name is Joker: u bludy GTH. *aana hai* . . . means *aana hai.* u've to com :-*

me: m not cnfm. jst waitin. waitin. n waitin :-(

After the kiss emoji from Joker's side, when 'me' did not type any message other than the waiting one, then Joker had, probably in frustration, asked, 'wru?' Looks like Joker

was calling her somewhere, but she for some reason didn't
want to meet him and had typed GTH. Go to Hell.

My heart beats with wild urgency. I don't have any
courage now to go further up the chat box. I am scared that
she'll know the computer was tampered with. I draw my
chair still further away from the computer.

She brings the milk in a small thermos. I stand up to
take the thermos from her hand.

'You have coffee and cups over there?'

'Ji . . . we have.'

She falls silent. I remain standing and gaze at her. The
lips are thin. Brown-coloured. Accentuated cheekbones.
Wheat complexion. Triangular-shaped forehead, and hair
that falls below the waist, braided into a single plait and
brought to the front. Below the nose and on the forehead,
fine drops of sweat glisten. From the ears, tiny flowers
dangle.

She says, '. . . and?'

I ask, '. . . and?'

She bows her head and moves away from the door.

She has worn a long kurta made from white cotton,
whose sleeves reach the wrist. The white cloth has been
embroidered with white threads. Her eyebrows are thick,
and on the forehead, between the brows, the space for bindi
is vacant.

She says, '. . . and?'

With a quick jerk of my head, I say, '. . . and? . . . there's
nothing else.'

She goes and opens the door.

I say, '. . . and . . . and yes . . . thanks!'

She beams.

I do not look back, but I do not hear the sound of the door closing either. Even after crossing the road and reaching the door of the library, the feeling that she hasn't closed the door lingers—for I know . . . I know that the door will remain open, standing wide to the street, and not close, till I walk back again and inside one more time. I stop abruptly at the entrance to the library and turn. From where I stand, the girl's window is visible. But I cannot discern any motion at the window. The curtain flutters like before.

Just that the other shutter is now open.

18

THE OLD WOMAN IS SILENT

'I have learned silence from the talkative, toleration from the intolerant, and kindness from the unkind; yet strange, I am ungrateful to these teachers.'

—Kahlil Gibran, *Sand and Foam*

Mangan's Ma is singing, which means she isn't always silent.

A while ago, she was humming a Sindhi song, of an unrelenting, unanswerable ache, *'Who has the guts to ask the sahib: how many errors you have made in creating this world!'* Now she is washing her doll in a bath mug. Putting baby soap in its hair. Rubbing its body in the frothy, soapy water. And singing all along, with sweet lugubriousness, a Sindhi wedding song,

Muhinjo son jo rupayo, Alla ri Alla
Muhinjo chandi jo rupayo, Alla ri Alla

Are got maa. Are got maa
(You're my gold rupee, Allah O Allah
You're my silver rupee, Allah O Allah
Hey bridegroom's mother. Hey bridegroom's mother)

In her trembling voice, with her cheeks flapping in and out, she had sung this song at every wedding to different tunes, beating a drum with a spoon. And, she had saved a special tune for herself. She thought, by singing at other weddings, she was practising for the final performance that she would give one day at Mangan's wedding. That Mangan who hadn't yet arrived in this world, and in whose wait she— Jalo—had already become Mangan's Ma.

No one could know when or how the bubbly, carefree Jalo sank into the quagmire of quietness. Words might have dried inside her, one by one. A dense laziness might have lodged itself inside, misleading the words or forbidding them from surfacing. One day she probably might have realized that in this world's cacophony, her own spoken words held no value. Now, her relationship with things was merely that of the sight with the scene.

While washing the doll, she always looked at its eyes. Lay it down, the eyes closed. Prop it up, they opened.

Every morning, at a fixed time, she placed it in the bathroom so that it could do its morning chores. Then she cleaned it. For breakfast, she'd make koki, and when she served it to Basar Mal with pickle and curd, she also made the doll sit next to him and hoped that Basar Mal would feed it a bite or two from his plate. And on days when she thought her doll preferred selmaani over koki, she tore the night's leftover roti into small pieces, fried them on an iron skillet, sprinkling some water till they hissed and spluttered, and then for many days, there would be only selmaani for breakfast. These days, she feels, her doll has developed a preference for the sweet lola—sensitive as always to her doll's gastronomic predilections.

She never talked to her doll. Never complained. Never criticized. A few times, however, she had spanked it, having become very angry. During the day, she kept her doll outside, on the edge of the road. That would be its playtime. One day, the doll was found ten metres away from its original place, lying on its stomach, splodged in mud. She brought it back home and, before washing it, gave it four tight slaps. Once when she felt the doll's language had acquired a strong, stubborn tone, even then she spanked it nicely.

But after every beating, she'd feel upset and hurt for a long time. She'd hope that the doll would come and pacify her, but in the end, weary of hoping anymore, she'd go to it herself, like a penitent child. And all this happened in complete silence—without speaking a word.

Once when she revealed these emotions to Basar Mal, the way he looked scared her, and she stopped confiding her feelings to him. She does not know when she ceased all conversation with her husband.

But Basar Mal often speaks to her about the land of the library and how certain people are hounding him to sell it. Every time after receiving a phone call from them, he comes and sits beside her and says, this time, he has been even more vociferous in refusing them, and they probably won't dare to call him again; but every fourth or fifth day, sometimes in the afternoon, at times in the evening, Basar Mal comes and sits beside her. And when he does, Mangan's Ma knows. And she also knows that Basar Mal regards her now as some mute statue. He comes and speaks to her but does not expect a response. She wants to respond, but then it seems utterly meaningless to her. What should she say? Should she say, sell the library? Or say, do not sell? Or say . . .

How does she see him? With the sight that has forgotten all her past, or the sight that has stowed away the past in a bottle, and either flung it into the sea or buried it in a slough like a treasure?

She lays the doll gently on the bed. Its eyelids close automatically. She removes her dupatta and covers it. Then, she takes the TV remote, her husband's spectacle case and her own, some ancient pens, and an old plastic rose and sits facing Basar Mal. Dipping a cloth in a mugful of water, she starts wiping each thing, one by one.

Basar Mal, as usual, has some old, yellowed papers in front of him, which he reads using the twofold magnification of his soda-bottle glasses and a magnifying glass. A drawing book lies beside him as always, with a blunt pencil and a worn-down eraser on it. The eraser dust from constant rubbing has been pinched and pelleted, and the pellets have been set neatly on the bedside.

After a while, he quits trying to read the land papers and gets busy with his drawing book. There is a half-finished sketch—legs walking and, with every leg, a stick. Bald heads above them. No bodies. Broken spectacles strewn, with their glass cracked. In the margin, scribbled in pencil:

We are the couplets of that ghazal
Whose rhyme has splintered
And fallen somewhere behind . . .

Quietly adding some more incompleteness on the sheet, a few more legs and sticks, he raises his head and lowers it again. 'There was a phone call,' he murmurs, 'They said they have much patience, and they can wait even 'til my death.'

How much did his eyes water while speaking it? Mangan's Ma wants to find out. She looks at his wet eyes, but all she can make out is his brimming pain she cannot bear to look at.

My eyes are like regions of the earth where water does not know if it should freeze or remain tears, Basar Mal thinks to himself.

'They said they know I'm old . . .' he says, his voice back down to that calm and tired patience, 'That I shouldn't have become this old—that I should have died long before—that someday they would crush me under a truck—that they would sprinkle petrol in my library and set fire—that they would burn the books—that their patience is wearing thin—that if I didn't sell them my land, someday they would bury me in this very land along with my books . . .'

Mangan's Ma, while wiping the spectacle case, unconsciously removes her own glasses and dunks them in the mug of water. Then starts wiping them with the cloth.

Basar Mal gets up and brings the Van Gogh packet from the closet. Inhaling it deeply he asks her, his voice thick with emotion, 'Jalo, remember this? . . .'

Without glasses, Mangan's Ma can't see anything clearly. She raises her head slightly once, then gets back to wiping her glasses. Basar Mal puts the packet under her nose. She turns her face away. He pulls a chair next to her and sits, a frail old man with passionate convictions.

'Ten years have passed refusing them,' he tells her, 'I've made up my mind that this time . . . this time I'll say *No* sternly, forcefully.'

It seems to Mangan's Ma as if someone is crying close by. In her hurried nervousness, she sticks the still-wet glasses to her eyes, trembling and shaking shambles inside, holding on to the wall. Slowly she reaches the room. Perhaps the doll flung the dupatta away in its sleep. Perhaps a mosquito bit it. Perhaps that woke the little doll and it has burst out crying.

Sitting alone, Basar Mal says to himself:

Just because no one borrowed a book from a library for eleven years, should it be destroyed?

—No, absolutely not.

Because a woman hasn't spoken to anyone for years, should she be killed?

—Absolutely not.

Because a man is now old and no longer useful, should he be thrown off a roof?

—Absolutely not.

No one has the right to take someone's land or life because it suits their logic of utility.

—Yes, absolutely. No one.

19

DIL KHUSH

'The old man seated on the bench picks up the red ball. The child is frightened by it and probably wonders—Do people in this world pick up other people's things like this?'

—Bhau Padhye, *Five Gardens*

Once again, today, there was a loud, angry disturbance at Dil Khush Sambose wallah's shop.

Such dramatic episodes are a frequent occurrence now. A crowd of thirty or thereabouts was usual in front of his shop even earlier, but never before had it felt like crowd trouble. Now even if five bunch together, a wave of fear washes the heart: *What could be happening there?* Perhaps Dil Khush also feels the same.

The five men seethed with rage. It was absolute madness and mayhem there. A wrestler-type rowdy had grabbed

Dil Khush by the collar. A chattering crowd had collected as is fitting for such scenes. Dil Khush was continuously apologizing for some crime he seemed to have committed. There was an urgent, frightened plead in his voice. He tried hard to calm them. But they crackled unrelentingly.

It looked like those rowdies had hit him.

Dil Khush's beard has greyed. But nobody has ever heard him swearing. In his shop, he has hung so many pictures that he seems to belong to every religion, every party, every faction. He addresses his customers as seth, raja, janab, sahib, big brother, sir, officer, my malik, my maula . . . and speaks to them so sweetly that even an unemployed worker sipping his tea would feel no less than a collector.

So it would definitely seem odd if someone grabbed Dil Khush by the throat. I walked up to them to intervene. Looking at me, some others also stepped in and tried pacifying those angry men. From the chatter going around, I learnt that five men had showed up for tea and snacks; one fellow fished out a whole lizard from his tea, and another found a cockroach in his vada. The cockroach finder had kept mum whereas the lizard fisher created a scene.

In a loud, rasping voice that shrilled like a siren, he ranted and raved about how after drinking Dil Khush's tea, people fall sick and how today, they finally found proof that the chap actually drops lizard in the tea!

Dil Khush was at his wits' end. He didn't know what to say. He would gape, sometimes at the fellow, and sometimes at the lizard that now lay on the bench, mushed in tea.

That irascible man's rant would not stop. Gratuitously gesturing, he repeatedly threatened Dil Khush that he would lodge a complaint with the Food Supply people—that he would get the shop sealed—that heaven knows for how long Dil Khush has been playing with people's health—that heaven knows how long it would continue—that he was a chameleon's chest—that he was a shrew's snout—that he was this—that he was that—

And Dil Khush was pleading with folded hands that no sahib, my seth, dear sir, it must have happened by accident, that at his place such negligence never occurred, and over and over again he kept gawking at the lizard.

Another person drinking tea saw the mushed lizard, he vomited on the ground, and in anger and disgust, threw away his tea glass and stormed out.

After this drama, which played out for a long time, there were no customers in his shop for a considerable period. This was unheard of in Dil Khush's shop. He went and sat on the protruding cash box and with the spoon started hitting his kettle hard. Clang—clang—clang. His glazed eyes were fixed like stones somewhere in the distance, while the hand continuously hammered.

'Tell me something,' he said, 'How hot will the tea be in this six-foot high kettle? And below it, twenty-four hours the gas stove burns. Won't the lizard melt in the kettle itself?'

I looked at him. He was speaking to me, but his eyes were fixed elsewhere. Distantly he went on, 'And the taphole of this kettle is not so big that a lizard can come out of it?'

'Point. But all this needed to be said in front of them?'
I chided him.

He became quiet. His hand was also tired. He gazed
at the pictures that graced the walls inside. In prayer or in
accusation, I do not know.

'Why didn't you open your mouth in front of them?'
I repeated.

'Look ré, in business one should not talk. Only listen.
That's it. Whatever work you can get done with joined
palms, that much is enough.'

While speaking, his lips may or may not have trembled,
his beard was surely shaking.

'It looks like they are after me.' He told it to me or to
himself, I do not know. But after that, in spite of my repeated
coaxing, he did not respond to any of my questions.

When the customers started trickling in again after a
while, he somewhat regained his composure. I left him and
went into the street to saunter further down.

Later, I learnt the Food Supply people had come the
same evening. They took samples of all the items in his
shop and the next day, they sealed the shop. The FSI
report stated:

Every product in the shop is a threat to health. There
is a lack of cleanliness, the shop is infested with germs, and
stale food is being sold.

* * *

Every morning Dil Khush stands beside his sealed shop.
When he is exhausted with his standing, he sits down.

Sometimes he runs to the city municipality, sometimes to the corporator.

The state of affairs remains unchanged. From trees, bird feathers fall like leaves. Ills rove the inauspicious streets at night. Bad news rises like a water fountain at the nearby Nehru Chowk.

Several days have passed, but his shop remains shut. That small kitchen is quiet. With a cold kettle, and the clutter all put away.

* * *

I saw Dil Khush for the last time in the library, seated in front of the old man. The old man was resting his head against the chair, his eyes fixed on the ceiling, while Dil Khush sobbed in his chair. Sensing me behind, Dil Khush rose in a flash, and left without so much as glancing at me.

I never saw him after that.

The old man still sat the same way. Body motionless, head back, eyes fixed on the ceiling. In the tiled roof, I don't know what he was staring at, I don't know what he searched for.

20

MY NAME IS 'I'

'Then I went back into the house and wrote, It is midnight. The rain is beating on the windows. It was not midnight. It was not raining.'

—Samuel Beckett, *Molloy*

:- I

She listened to my silence and giggled. I sat with bowed head. Before that, she had wandered slowly through my hair with her fingers. Before that, she had perched before me, while I watched her lip tremble. Before that, she had bathed, and a water drop on her forehead was about to roll down. Before that, she was stretching herself, and her body, like some medieval ruin, was cracking and crashing. From the ruin, each time a brick would fall with a thud, turn into dust, scatter.

Before that, she had asked, 'Do you know how to love?'

Even before her asking, I had declared, 'No, I am a man.'

Before my declaration, she had tickled my cheeks with her eyelids.

And before that, I had shaken her dangling earrings by blowing softly.

Her earlobes quivered like the quivering flame of the lamp kept at the doorstep.

:-*

She said, 'and . . .'

I said, 'and . . . and I want to stick to your forehead like a water drop, I am the avatar of sun that has descended just to live on this forehead, I am the orb of moon living in your eyes—do you have any idea that I am your eyesight . . .'

:-)

She said, 'and . . .'

I said, 'and . . . and I am that lone mole on your nape, like the lone star hanging in the sky in complete darkness that defers its fall time after time in expectation of another star . . . from your earlobe I hang as an earring, and in your long tresses as a lock that you deliberately put off untangling . . . I am an imaginary desert and you a real oasis, I should merge in you—that every particle of my sand would transform into a little green leaf, a fistful of sand would turn into a palmful of water . . . I am an ancient touch that moistens in its own sensation.'

:-0

She said, 'and . . .'

I said, 'and . . . and you are a forest, I camouflage in you as greenery. You are a river, I flow in you like a wave. You are a clump of trees, I hide in you like a velvet rabbit. You are a distance—you draw away from me all the time. You are a closeness—I draw you into me every time.'

She said, 'and . . .'

I said, 'and . . . and your every tress is a long street that I walk through—where I hope to walk all my life.'

She said, 'and . . .'

I said, 'and . . .'

She said, 'yes, and . . .'

I lapsed into silence. She stood right in front of me. A thermos in hand. From the open thermos, the curtain of steam had stretched stiff in between us. Her freshly washed hair emanated the intoxicating fragrance of coffee. In the yellow of her face, her coffee-coloured lips shone. She lilted deliciously towards the bookrack, took out a book, turned back, and beamed gloriously at me.

And said, 'and . . .'

:-|

But I remained silent.

She listened to my silence and giggled. I sat with bowed head. She was stretching herself, and her body, like some medieval ruin, was cracking and crashing. From the ruin, each time a brick would fall with a thud, turn into dust, scatter.

The walls of the ruin had, before crashing, suspended in air for some time. They had suspended in expectation. Like a broken leaf from a tree, they had long wavered in the air

before falling to the ground. They had wavered, expecting
me—

While I had sat with bowed head.

She giggled again. I raised my head. Within a moment,
she transformed from the girl of the yellow window into
Imbelo. Then laughing, giggling, she turned into a bird. A
chirping, giggling bird.

Chirping, wings flapping, she whirred close to my head.
I could feel the wind of her claws on my cheeks and its heat.

Even now I can feel her above my throbbing head—at
this window where I stand looking at the window across
the street. Its yellow shutters are open, the curtain swinging
like before. The latticed flowers are silent like they were,
and no face peeks from behind them. Sometime before,
there was a glimpse of her, now there's nothing. She had
seen me standing, and she had even returned my smile.
Sometime before, she had wandered among the books in
this room of the library, lifting each book delicately, turning
and glancing at me, then putting it back. She had worn the
same white kurta, long sleeves, white embroidery.

Then changing into a delightful bird named Giggle,
she had flown away and sat on the parapet of the yellow
window . . . The rain beat on my window.

I retire to my chair. It is not raining.

* * *

The old man hasn't come in yet. He told me that he'd
be late today. Suddenly, I hear scuffing and scraping in

the gravel outside. I turn and see two men standing at the library door. Behind them, some workers are unloading cement bags from a small truck. The two men come in urgently and ask for the old man. I tell them he isn't in yet. They hesitate for a moment, but then one of them tells the workers standing outside to bring in the cement bags.

The workers rush thickly in, depositing the gunny bags against the wall beside the books. There are at least thirty to forty cement bags.

'You asked Uncle about this, no?' I want confirmation.

'Yes, Uncle himself told us.'

A cloud of dust rises sluggishly every time a bag is dumped. When I can't bear the hot, dusty smell anymore, I come out and, moving to the corner, light a cigarette. In the slanting late afternoon sun, the gravelly-sandy dumps strewn everywhere are clearly visible. Dust hangs above the open compound, too. I wonder what these Mool Chandanis are up to, piling their materials here.

The two men have followed me outside and are constantly barking instructions at the workers, their voices louder even than the jarring thuds and thumps.

I peep inside. The room is choked in a pall of grey dust. I am upset. I am angry. Why did the old man let these fellows keep the bags inside? With such effort we had cleaned the books and racks. Now they are filthy again.

21

THE OLD MAN'S STORY

'What I remember is a picture floating around out there outside my head. I mean, even if I don't think it, even if I die, the picture of what I did, or knew, or saw is still out there. Right in the place where it happened.'

—Toni Morrison, *Beloved*

While urinating in the bathroom, Basar Mal Jetharam Purswani feels for the first time that he is going to die. Such vulnerability while pissing! It surprises him. And frightens him. After much persuasive pressure, he finally gets some relief. But now, his heart begins to beat violently, his legs shake uncontrollably, his forehead soaks with sweat, and he repeatedly feels that he will collapse. Clasping the tap, he sits there down. Every joint in his body shudders. The fear in him gallops unbounded.

He remains a good half hour squatting this way and when at last he straightens himself up, he finds he has a weird pain in his knees from sitting too long. He picks his stick by the door and slowly shambles back to his place. Leaning his head against the wall shuts his eyes.

The evening has deepened. Mangan's Ma is outside washing the road.

Basar Mal looks out the window. The moon is lucent in the darkening sky. The girl whom he had kissed many years ago under a guava tree—who still popped out from between books—whose laughter he could still hear from inside the thermos—who, on opening the closet, seemed to topple over him and snorting 'hunh!' disappear to a side—she had shown her displeasure at the moon for rising early one evening many years ago.

Memory would fluster him in this irrational manner he hadn't imagined!

But despite the present pain, despite his tormenting moments of remembrance and erasure, he cannot stop himself from wondering, *didn't the moon rise early the night he returned to Larkana?* With unseemly haste, he fetches the sheaf of papers he had left unfinished the other day and opens—the scarred folds have been taped carefully—at the page on which he had walked away from the Karachi refugee camp—the turbulent, fiercely eventful memories of an eighteen-year-old culled out in sections and neatly laid out on paper:

* * *

No matter how long it took God to make this world, it didn't take the world any time to crumble.

Before leaving Larkana, we had padlocked our doors and bolted all windows shut to prevent rain, animals, and thieves from entering, and although we knew the house would no longer call us, we had turned back to look at it. We thought at least there would be a chance to return if we hoped.

But the house had been destroyed in a matter of hours. The windows and doors had been uprooted. The furniture had disappeared. Even cheap pictures hanging on the walls were not spared. The clothes we had left behind were gone, along with their almirahs. There used to be an enormous chandelier in the drawing room. I remember my father had procured it fondly from Tehran. Now, only its long iron shaft remained pendent from the ceiling.

I lay down under it until dark before proceeding to the eastern edge of the city where the madrasa was. I was to meet Jaam below its yellow window before sunrise and take her to Shahdadkot. That was the plan, and the promise. The moon rose early that night. But I waited for dawn.

A rising sun is a symbol of hope in the art of different world cultures. But there is nothing more indifferent and pitiless than the art of nature. I was stricken by grief and despair, but across the mud wall of the madrasa, the sunrise was glorious—so glorious—that anyone's mouth would open, as if by pure reflex, shaped to a clichéd praise, for the artistry of creation. People usually cannot imagine that an extremely delightful sunrise could be a synonym for somebody's personal disappointment, but I know I will always loathe the rising of the sun.

That day as I waited, with everything gilded by the morning sun, the story of my life went headlong in another direction.

No one came to that forsaken madrasa except the two of us. I took out my trademark white handkerchief, embroidered on three sides, from my sling bag and tied it to the window grille so that if Jaam saw it even from a distance, she would recognize it and immediately understand that the fluttering sign of love on the deserted window that only our love had inhabited, was meant for her. Like me, she knew no other person apart from us considered this window worthy of bearing a sign of love.

The morning was hot and bright. No matter how desolate the madrasa was, it wasn't safe in broad daylight. Facing the yellow window some half a kilometre away began the forest. I hid myself in the darkness of a clump of trees. The yellow window was clearly visible from there. Against the backdrop of this wait, I waited for the afternoon because, in those brief moments of madness, I had made up my mind that I should go directly to her house in Resham Street and call on her, though the calling I realized meant an alternative death.

The afternoons of Larkana are hot and sad. The streets silent, deserted, damned. People drowse in their houses, shopkeepers in their shops. Those, who don't have a house or a shop, drowse under a tree at the edge of the street or the public square. I moved stealthily like a daytime thief from one neighbourhood to another, passing by the dozing, drowsing people.

What a fool I was! Not once did I think her family also would have left the city like mine. Or perhaps something untoward would have happened. But was a Larkana without Jaam imaginable even in my most vulnerable moments?

I had no sooner entered her house than my vague, shadowy fears materialized before me like some tormenting spirit. That place had been completely ravaged, looted, and torched. There were wet blood stains in the courtyard. Amoebic patches of fire-hot soot stuck to the walls and the ceiling. Torn clothes lay strewn. Utensils, canisters, boxes, and trunks were all mercilessly thrown around.

I was living the most frightful moment of my life, but my desire to discover any sign of Jaam dwarfed all fears as I searched, steadily and deliberately, the entire house, almirahs, niches, alcoves, any place that was capable of concealing a human life. However, the scene of destruction bore no signs of her, carrying mutely just the burn marks from the blaze.

Squatting on the floor, head in my hands, I broke down and wept but eventually fell asleep with spent despair.

The deepened night rife with screaming crickets frightened me into waking. My eyelids were swollen from crying. Jaam would say tears have glue, and that's why eyelids stiffen. Blinking fresh tears, I hurried out of the house, anxious to reach the clump of trees half the city away. The rioters could appear from anywhere. I knew that if they saw me, they would strip me naked, and on noticing I hadn't been circumcised, they would kill me or rape me first before killing me. Only two things could save me at that point. One, I should cut off the roll of skin overhanging my penis, but I didn't have the required tools or time. Second, I should commandeer my two feet to be agile so as to reach the clump at breakneck speed.

Frankly, I had just one option.

I saw sticks lying in the courtyard. The people of the house had probably used them for self-defence. They had let go of their sticks while losing their lives or thrown them away while running away defeated. The victorious never throw their stick. I picked up a sturdy stick, weighing its strength in my hand and galloped fast into the streets.

Clumps of trees stretched across the dense forest. The trees skirting the edge of the forest threw up their trunks in the sky and, along with shrubs and vines, made a good hideaway. I decided to take refuge there, going in search of Jaam every day, as long as it was needed, to glean any bit of information about her.

The following day, I walked about the neighbourhood of Resham Street, scratching the drying-up blood with my stick, looking at lamenting women, peeping through the freshly broken walls of deserted Hindu houses. Heedless in my grief, I didn't realize that it had fallen dark. I hastened towards the forest and knocked into a man. I froze; my grip on the stick tightened. But he spoke in a very friendly voice, asking about my well-being, embracing me, all the while assuming that I was Mehmood, the stick-fighter, who was supposed to arrive in Larkana that evening. I was badly in need of a hug and a pat, and even if the man who called himself Abbas had other reasons, I was grateful. His voice had such an effect on me that like a robot, I went along with him. I realized he hadn't seen Mehmood before. He took me to his friends. They were all rioters. They had probably burned the houses in the neighbourhood, including Jaam's house.

I made an outrageously risky choice of joining them as Mehmood, the stick-fighter. I hadn't even beaten a dog with a stick in my life, and here I was walking with them, wielding a stick, as if I was a dreaded stick-fighter. I had to take my chance to find out about Jaam. In the prevailing chaos and panic, I realized I could manage to go along with this guise. Encouraged by it, and driven by my only purpose in life, I accompanied Abbas to dangerous places where henchmen congregated. They swaggered with swords at their waists, fully-loaded firearms in their pockets, and oil-fed sticks in their hands. I heard that they were holding captive many Hindu girls. A tiny seed of hope sprouted in my heart: Would Jaam be among them? Could someone tell me the bad that happened in her house? Who was responsible for that?

Jaam lived in a grandiose three-storey house on Resham Street, also called Silk Street. There were extremely prosperous Sindhi Hindus living in Larkana. The wealth was preserved, amassed, and multiplied for centuries from generation to generation, and the families passed on their businesses and shrewd financial acumen as also secret tricks of the trade. Dada Parsaram was one such affluent Sindhi Hindu, greatly respected for not just his wealth but his philanthropy too, and so well-known that you had to only ask for the direction to his house, and someone would gladly take you to 'Sukh Nivas', his abode of happiness, in Nanak Mohalla.

The Muslims who came from Hindustan at the time of Partition were called muhajirs. They had been, like the Sindhi Hindus here, harassed and tortured. They had, like us, lost everything in the riots of Hindustan, where Hindus were emphatically announcing their presence and their hatred towards the Muslims.

We weren't afraid of the local Muslims. We were afraid of the muhajirs. They were complete strangers and were taking out their anger and violence on us for having been persecuted there. They hated the Sindhi prosperity and feared that powerful people like Dada

Parsaram would jeopardize their political aspirations by winning the election.

One such muhajir was Mr Syed, who had arrived from Lucknow. He was a leader of the Muslim League in Hindustan. As soon as the possibility of an Islamic state of Pakistan became a reality, he shifted to Karachi and then moved to Larkana.

Syed and some others wanted as much land in their possession as was possible through subterfuge and to get it legally in their names before something like a refugee board could become operational, and before the legal settlement of property and wealth commenced. They manipulated and made the legal papers look as though the Hindu families had sold their properties legitimately before leaving.

Pakistan had been carved. Whoever had the ownership of most land and property was to be the most powerful. The rapacious Syed's work picked up speed. Of course, there were rival gangs who hindered the process. So, he not only roped in the wild young henchmen, arse-lickers, and creeps but also lured into his fold the poor Muslims of the region.

No other male had eyes bluer than Syed.

They say in our Sindh, 'Only the lucky ones are able to see men having blue eyes.' Once upon a time if Mahmud Ghaznavi had seen these blue eyes, he would have surely left Ayaz and embosomed Syed. If he had been in Babur's court, then instead of that Kabuli kid, Syed's name would have appeared in *Tuzk-e-Babri*. If he

had stood in the streets of Fergana, old men indulging
in *bacha bazi* or boy play would have clawed him away.
If he had been a Sufi, his murshid would have taken
him to paradise. From Muhammad Ghori to Akbar to
Aurangzeb to Bahadur Shah Zafar, be it a badshah, be
it a faqir, there is a long history of lust and adoration in
this geographical region for boys with blue eyes.

I heard Syed kept many catamites himself in
his entourage.

He spoke in such clear and sweet Urdu as though a
bag of sugar. He considered himself a great disciple of
Allama Iqbal and his poetry. But from the inside, he was
a bastard. For years, he had dreams of becoming a leader
of the Muslim League in Pakistan.

The killings that had taken place in Larkana in the
past few days, were they Syed's doing? Could a man with
a sugary tongue kill? Could a murder be etched with the
same delicateness as a poem? It was beyond my thinking to
clear away these doubts. But I was certain that the person
who had dared us politely the other night, brandishing a
sword and whose poetic threats had made father describe
him as 'an elegant, well-mannered terror', was Syed.

There was no news of Mehmood, and my guise
as that stick-fighter was working well. It must have
satisfied my ego that not even my reflection in the
mirror was able to recognize me, which, of course, was
to be shattered in the coming days.

Mustafa was Syed's foe, his competitor, who also
wanted to seize as much land as possible and become

a future leader of Pakistan. He not only had a large gang but also had the implacable Baloch on his side. There were clear tensions between the two warlords, especially over the control of territories. Mustafa had laid claim to Resham Street and five other localities. Resham Street where half the Hindu money as well as the second largest mansion in Larkana sat. I came to know that Syed acquiesced but not before secretly sending for a dangerous stick-fighter to break Mustafa's head. His plan was to kill Mustafa and place the blame on Sobho Gianchandani, who was a communist and worked for communal peace. Sobho went to the Hindu homes with his team to convince them not to leave their land. 'Don't sever ties with the soil of Sindh,' he pleaded, 'If courage is shown, Hindus can progress and prosper here in this country.'

Now how could Syed permit such a thing? I am sure if Syed was afraid of anyone, it was Sobho Gianchandani. That fellow was just twenty-six or twenty-seven, thin, wiry, who could be blown away with a mere puff, but so honest that you couldn't buy him, and so truthful and learned that you couldn't beat him in an argument. Every political party is afraid of such a man. I heard he had more books than Syed, not to forget he had studied in Rabindranath Tagore's Shantiniketan, where Tagore called him 'a living man who has come from Mohenjo-daro'. (Mohenjo-daro, or the mound of the dead, is in Sindh.) Syed was fiercely and openly hostile towards Sobho: hatching plots, and refusing to accept Sobho's popularity.

The knowledge I gained from the streets was more than I had acquired in my entire life 'til now. The sharp effluvium of hatred, greed, and intolerance left me gasping for breath. All of a sudden, I got to look at a world where, behind every beautiful form, there was a stench—smirking, sneering, malicious in its filthy odours.

One of my cached disbeliefs is that I, Basar Mal Jetharam Purswani, who was born in Larkana, who spent his life's eighteen years in these streets like a vagabond, who thought he knew every part of the city, and every guava tree, was, in reality, so ignorant. I didn't know anything about my own city: the intrigues, the activities, and the intentions spreading like poison in the bodies. I was only a lover. There is no one more heedless than a lover. No one more focused.

Just imagine you were me, and I told you a few incredible stories about the dark side of your city while taking you around your own city, those you didn't even have an inkling about. How would you feel? You wouldn't believe in the stories, but believe me, disbelief is the name of the first stairstep into the black well of disappointment.

Instead of saying anything more, I will relate a story I heard on the street. It was recounted to me by Abbas, whom, I came to know, Syed loved not just for his skill at sniffing stories but also for his perky butt. An account in which the girl, though not called Jaam is, I know, Jaam:

'You have asked me three times, and, all three times, I have sworn that neither Syed's hand nor mine was in the split blood at the house on Resham Street. I swear again by Muqaddas Quran Shareef. Mehmood Miyan, this is not our territory. It is Mustafa's territory. You know him? He is the kind of motherfucker—well, how do I say?—think of him as someone who puts his finger in his own asshole to delight in the smell, like he were some Mughal emperor seated on his throne enjoying the scent of a flower. He had planned it for days. I got a whiff of it; I told you I am an expert at sniffing other people's stories, and at Syed's behest, I began to watch him.

It turned out that he always had a crush on Seth Dayal Das' daughter. Whenever he saw her, he would declare his love for her and pour his soul out, but the girl didn't care two hoots about him. On the contrary, she humiliated him by throwing his flowers in the gutter. So, the lover Mustafa was also eager to take revenge on her. He vaguely knew that the girl was entangled with some Sindhi Hindu boy, but who that son of a bitch was, he couldn't find out. Otherwise, he would have slit the boy's throat first. The attack on Dayal Das' house was not for money but for the girl. His plan was to kidnap Dayal Das' daughter when the Hindus of the

Resham Street were to be struck one last time, and then, drive away her family to Hindustan. In the chaos and panic, the family wouldn't be able to do anything. He would acquire not just the girl but all of the Seth's wealth. What a bastard! He planned and prepared for three months, and no one got no whiff of it.

It was the night the moon rose early, when Mustafa, along with a handful of Baloch, attacked the house. But the Seth was too clever by half. He had, sensing the pulse of the city, secured the place with ten bodybuilder-type gunmen, who shot half the men while Mustafa managed to escape. He returned three hours later with fifty Baloch. The Baloch are ruthless. They brush their teeth with the muzzle of their guns. This time they did not enter from the front, but sneak-attacked from the backside of the house. They broke a part of the back wall and quietly penetrated, one by one. The Seth and his servants were busy filling sacks with all the accumulated wealth, hidden away in remote corners of the mansion: cash, jewellery, gold biscuits, and gemstones. The guards were falsely drawn into thinking that the trouble had been averted, and they were also hastily helping them stash the wealth. Perhaps the Seth's plan was to leave for Hindustan before dawn. People say he had hired motor cars for Karachi. Mehmood Miyan, I feel Mustafa knew all of this beforehand, and that's why he did not delay his second attack. When the Baloch entered through the broken back wall, all people inside were unarmed. The

mayhem began. All ten guards were dragged to the yard
and beaten with sticks before ripping their bodies open
with the long blade of the sword. Tell me, do the Baloch
ever spare anyone? They shot the Seth and his family
multiple times. When the servants tried to escape, the
Baloch chased them to the backstreet and killed them,
and dragged their dead bodies like dogs to the yard.
More kafirs were killed on Resham Street that night
than in the entire Larkana on any night. No, no, here I
am wrong. Once, as many were killed, twelve hundred
years ago, when our magnificent Arab commander-in-
chief and our greatest ancestor Muhammad bin Qasim
set foot on the land of Sindh. They had also delighted in
butchering thousands of kafirs. I feel so utterly thrilled,
I get goose bumps just thinking about the bravery of
my great ancestor! I didn't know about this history at
all. How would I, an unread asshole, who's never seen
a book in his life? It is the kindness of Syed Sahib that
a little knowledge has come my way. Ah, how with
great joy he tells the stories of our ancient ancestors,
how because of them our great religion was introduced
in this part of the world, and our race flourished! Shall
I tell you one more interesting thing? It's funny how I
thought Pakistan was created only recently, and it was
all Hindustan earlier. Syed Sahib says the making of
Pakistan began twelve centuries ago, on the day when
our greatest ancestor, may Allah rest his soul in peace,
Muhammad bin Qasim had set foot here. I am so proud
that the history of our country, Pakistan, the bestest in

the world, is centuries old! It doesn't matter if it found its identity only a few days earlier. Syed Sahib tells me that even Jinnah Sahib, who defeated the English and Hindus to give Pakistan freedom, says that Muhammad bin Qasim is the world's first Pakistani. Now Syed Sahib wouldn't lie to me, would he?

Oh, you're still stuck with that Seth's story? No, it's not over yet. Actually, the story took a new turn after that.

So the chief of the Baloch was Salim Baloch. He caught the cunningness of that trickster Mustafa. When the Baloch were slaughtering the ten bodybuilder-type guards in the yard, Mustafa, along with his two boys, had gone to that part of the mansion where like frightened sparrows, the women of the Dayal Das household were hiding. Mustafa stuffed some cloth in the Seth's daughter's mouth, tied her hands and feet and, turning her almost into a bundle, shut her in a small room at the back of the house. He locked the door so that she remained safely away from the sight of the Baloch. I think Mustafa's plan was to wait until all the looting was over, the killings quietened, and the Baloch left the mansion, and, then, discreetly come back to pick up Dayal Das' daughter. But the Baloch got a whiff of his vile wish when a weeping Dayal Das' wife pleaded with Salim Baloch, 'Kill me, but please leave my daughter!' Salim was surprised. He asked, 'What daughter? Here there's no one so young to be your daughter.' Salim turned the mansion upside down, searching for the daughter, and Mustafa was exposed. One look at the fairy-like divine daughter of Dayal Das and Salim Baloch's intentions turned evil. This is what Mustafa had probably feared. Salim reneged on his promise and now insisted on taking the Seth's daughter, along with half the loot. When that scoundrel Mustafa protested, he was beaten up and barely escaped with his life. When the Baloch finally emerged after setting fire to the house, how many sacks they lugged on their backs, filled with the plunder of the house, and how many kafir dead bodies they loaded in two pushcarts, like cats and dogs! And slung on Salim Baloch's shoulder, the cruellest of them, a six-footer animal, was Dayal Das' daughter, writhing like a fish out of water.

And what else would he have done except for clawing away at her? My soul trembles thinking of this, and I bow down to my Allah and thank Him that He did not make us a woman. What can we do, Mehmood Miyan? She was born in the wrong place at the wrong time in the wrong religion. But, no, why should I think of her? If one has to protect their religion, then mercy has to be kept at a distance—fair enough, huh? *Allah Nigahban*! So long!'

Disbelief engulfed me as I listened to his story of the slaughter, plunder, lust, and destruction. I went to squat in the mud on the bank of the Rice Canal, covered by soot, dead black, disappointed. I didn't understand whether the wind blowing over the canal that divided Larkana into two parts was colder or my body, which was like a dead body. Numbed, I walked for miles, directionless. Like pebbles in a tin canister, pieces of my broken spirit clanged inside my body to the beat of my footfalls, playing over the monstrosity encore after encore.

Did I still have a glimmer of hope that I would glimpse Jaam and, like the hero of an epic, save her? Was she still in Larkana? I couldn't know. It was becoming increasingly dangerous to live in the guise of a stick-fighter. I was an ordinary Sindhi youth, not so famous that people in my city would recognize me, but I had spent my childhood here, and there was always a lurking danger of bumping into a familiar face. I also knew that if Abbas and the others saw through my disguise, they would kill me with my own stick in a most humiliating and ruthless manner at some public square. I hoped and lived. Maybe it was my Allah who had kept me here.

A few days later, Abbas' fine ability to sniff stories added some more to my knowledge:

'I told you, didn't I, that Salim Baloch carried away the girl. From then on, his bad days began. It seems that night, Salim carried not Dayal Das' daughter on his shoulder but his misfortune. In his zeal and preoccupation to control that girl, he delayed the distribution of the loot among his men, which led to a revolt in his group. To tell you frankly, this was just an excuse, as the fire of hatred against him had already been kindled. The dissents needed just an opportunity, which Salim, heedless in his love for that girl, gifted them himself. I heard that his group attacked him in the middle of the night, and Salim answered with his gun, killing four people. Then, with the girl, he rode away to the hills of Kutte-Ji-Qabar on his famous stallion. The Baloch followed him a long distance, and kept firing at him. No one knows if he died or not, but he was certainly hit. His screams were heard near Kutte-Ji-Qabar, although the story goes that he managed to escape. Good for him! Had he been caught, his gang would have hung his dead body at some square in Larkana. And that girl? Brother, no one knows what happened to the Seth's cherubic daughter. Some people say she was also shot, but no one saw her dead body. Some say she ran away with Salim, but to rescue a girl from the clutches of the Baloch is like putting one's hand in the lion's mouth to snatch its meat. If you ask me, she was quite capable of impersonating a young boy and, in the commotion, sneaking herself out. There are as many opinions as there are people! I personally think she lives here in Larkana hiding somewhere.'

Surprisingly, Abbas was more than eager to help me in my search. A strange love that he showed, holding my hand affectionately, almost dragging me away to places where he thought we could find Jaam. I began to understand Abbas' intentions when I found him knocking on the doors of the houses where Hindu girls, kidnapped by Syed's gang, were kept. I came to know that the girls were kept, not in one place, but in different houses across the city, and almost every girl had been claimed by some rich Muslim. Some of them were kept as maids, some as half-wives. From Khichi Mohalla to Aliabad Mohalla to Goth Suba Khan Nuhani, the places spread across the city, but those distances proved insufficient to exhaust Abbas and his enthusiasm, although in every place, he found disappointment. I began to understand that Abbas was himself a lustful man, and I was just an excuse.

I had gained Abbas' friendship and confidence, and he had taken me to meet Syed. The first time Syed saw me, he had asked me to turn around. I did not know what he wanted to see. But a touch on my butt made me jump and stand away. An electric shock bolted through my body as I became aware of his intent. I was so scared that I could not even show my fear.

Sometimes fear lodges so deep inside that, against our wishes, we start dancing to the other person's tunes. The inner fear is so damn hypnotizing!

Abbas and the others were living in evicted Hindu houses, and he easily convinced me to stay with him. Not out of fear but love, I gladly became Abbas' captive. When he grabbed my hand and pulled me towards him, it was like Shams taking Rumi's hand, or Auliya holding Khusrau's, or Shah Inayat holding Bulleh's hand. As the magic of his touch slowly enveloped my whole existence, my every attempt to get away from him proved useless. If he had, with his loving hands, dragged me into the fire of Hell, I might have given him that pleasure, too.

At all times the watchful, loving eyes of Abbas were on me. I became lazy like a man in his in-laws' house. I became a tad careless. And this turned out to be my biggest mistake. Slowly, I understood that they were playing games with me. Why did I take a keen interest in Dayal Das' daughter? Abbas was beginning to be suspicious. After all, he was an expert at sniffing stories. I'm sure he didn't know where Dayal Das' daughter was. It was simply to prevent me from leaving the town that he had baited me with the idea of Jaam being in Larkana. Why would he have done that?

Perhaps Syed had caught on to my identity, and Abbas was merely a guard and keeper on Syed's orders. I was beginning to have an uneasy feeling that I was being watched. Abbas or someone would run into me, or prowl close by on some pretext. Until now, I considered myself a guest in Abbas' place, but in reality, I was under house arrest and so cleverly under house arrest that I did not even feel I was a prisoner. It was the cunning brilliance of Syed. A few of his boys had casually begun making snide remarks that I would become Syed's personal property, and that he would kill me once he had his fill of me.

More than death, I became scared of Syed and the way he creepily looked at me. That imperceptible linger of his hand on my butt haunted me. Ya Allah! Death was a far better option. Each day was a nightmare. I was so consumed with being scared and terrorized that it seemed I was either waiting to be killed or raped by Syed.

The clump was still a safe haven. In fact, I hadn't gone back there ever since I started living with Abbas. No one had sniffed it yet. I looked for an opportunity to sneak into the shadow of my familiar trees, which presented itself very soon. We were brushing our teeth with neem twigs outside the house when the news came that Mustafa's dead body was lying, drenched in blood, at the Miro Khan square. Throwing our neem *datuns*, we all ran towards the square. It suddenly struck me that I could leave the premises! In the commotion of the brutal killing, when all eyes were averted from me, I slipped away unnoticed and, grateful for that death, ran like the wind pausing only after reaching the clump.

I spent the next ten days in the forest opposite the madrasa.

During those days, trees were my closest companion, my closest confidants. They taught me the skill of living alone. Trees, even while living in clusters, render a feeling of aloneness. The collectivity of trees is similar to that of humans. The collectivity of being alone in a crowd.

My life became a confluence of conflicting situations. I was brave but also very scared. I was hopeful, but also dejected. I waited, yet I was filled with indifference. I was hungry, but my stomach felt full all the time. I was thirsty, but from the inside, I was very wet. I was restrained, but my actions belied craziness. I was calm yet took out my anger each day, banging on trees. These were all obverses. And my life was a dedication to contradictions in those days.

My Jaam was not in Larkana. There was no point staying there any longer. Had I stayed, I would have surely been killed at the hands of Syed. I felt guilty and defeated, but the truth is I tried. The streets of Larkana are witness to the fact that Basar Mal Jetharam Purswani had tried, really tried, even risking his life, but he was helpless. He was helpless because before writing the story of his fate, God had dipped the tip of His pen in poo.

On the madrasa window, the embroidered handkerchief ruffled boldly in the light morning breeze, in glory of love. There was no 'Why are you leaving so early, Basar Mal?' and no sulking as I prepared to return and began packing my everything—some clothes, a blanket to ward off the cold, a few loose papers, a pencil, small eats, and a water bottle. Then a sulk and a snort, and some laughter, words filled with love, love filled with silence, the hundred-page letter and the soil shrouding it, the dearly loved madrasa, its yellow window, and that wait, the size of the universe, tied to the window in a white handkerchief embroidered on three sides, also the street that went from my house to the madrasa, streets that went from any point of the city to her house, indolence that coiled like a lazy python on the streets, mornings and evenings that looked always like afternoons, shade of the guava tree, sap of the leaf, fragrance of the fruit.

I stacked them neatly in my memory and in my oblivion to carry them the way we carry our souls inside us.

And our dead.

Before leaving, I took water from the invisible river of tears flowing within, in the city of faith that flowers hope, and poured it on the earth of Sindh as *arghya*, a libation: O motherland, let this land remain wet so that the hope of my return keeps feeding, that you had told me, my Sindhland, the patch of earth irrigated with tears blisters like burned skin.

* * *

And that was all. While crossing the Mirpur Khas border, the police had trawled through his things but couldn't find anything. The heavy weight of his eighteen years had borne him across! Dear Jhulelal!

He folds the sheets as carefully as his shaky hands can allow him. He could never afterwards go back to his other side. He only recalls someone telling him that the rioters had seized the madrasa. And the girl Jaam—he could never bring himself to accept the fact that she was actually gone!

'Becoming fragrance, has she settled in the guava?'
'Or has she become the fragrance of guava in my life?'

There is no logic bigger than love—and that is all he can say.

22

THE OLD MAN'S STORY

'As a bird is numbed when its gaze glides on a black snake, the terror benumbed the senses. He turned back to look and realized that what he had presumed was clearly true.'

—U.R. Ananthamurthy, *Samskara*

Basar Mal's heart races as if the throttle was jammed down. Does it go faster than the events that streak past once again in his mind? He can't tell.

That roar of the Partition, with all its fury, turmoil, and grief, had swept him out to another land, a new world in which he re-lived and re-loved. And now the memories have re-entered his life like a diurnal army of tormentors.

For many years since Partition, his soul was a faraway city hewed out of a childhood dream calling his name.

That city of faith slowly turned into a city of illusion. For many years, he collected and recollected his memories. Those were slowly swept to a forgotten corner in his heart. Why, then, is he dusting his past? Why is he thinking of a girl, who for him ceased to be more than sixty years ago, at a time when he suffers the worst pain, receives death threats, and when the danger of being stripped of his land looms? Is this memory his delayed apology? Apology to the girl? Apology to Jalo? Apology to his parents? Apology to those long years when such memories lurked inside him like hidden lesions?

He does not even know if his parents are dead or alive. He tries to remember the last thing he said to his mother.

In the Karachi refugee camp, the burning regret of leaving Jaam had ruined his hunger. He and his mother were awake lying on their newspapers, with her trying to make him eat and he refusing. Then, he lost his cool and blew up at her. His mother nervously turned and lay quiet without speaking a word after that.

'Never shout at your mother who is urging you to eat, or else she will fall asleep with her back to you, and your rotis will taste like sand for a lifetime.'

He rises and goes to the window crying quietly, 'We are memory bombs. When we explode, we explode inward.'

The dark air is humid, and the stars are coming out. Mangan's Ma is still outside, washing the street with her pipe, singing softly to herself. Her plastic doll sleeps on the bed, wrapped in a dupatta. She put kohl under its eyes too, when she darkened hers.

He looks around the room. The great artists look back at him from their photo frames. He thinks, 'My room teems with the dead. Dead writers dead painters dead musicians.'

Presently he pats his chest to rein in his breath and assuage the pain.

Dil Khush had come last evening. After a long while. Those people managed to close down his shop using subterfuge. Now they want to open a hotel there.

Propped on his stick, the old man clacks his way out to the front. Mangan's Ma has created quite a slush of mud on the street. Everyone is familiar with her penchant for washing the street and is probably exasperated with the muck she creates. An autorickshaw passes by, scrunching on the wet street. From the slush puddle, water splashes. On the dry road ahead, the mud-caked tracks of the tyres stretch into the distance.

Dil Khush had a black contusion under his eye. He sat in front of him, sobbing and telling his story. First, they had repeatedly instigated mayhem in front of his shop so that people stayed away from his place. Next, to break his customer base, they had dropped a lizard in the tea and continued to besmirch his reputation. Then, they had the shop sealed. They had been asking him to sell his land for nearly a year. Now, when the desperate chap was willing to sell his shop, they weren't giving him the right price.

All through, Basar Mal felt it was not Dil Khush who sat in front of him. It was he. It was not Dil Khush who cried, but he. It was not Dil Khush's beard pulled in broad daylight, but his. Not Dil Khush who was caught by his

collar and abused. Not Dil Khush who was threatened
with the humiliation of *kesh-katal*—that abominable act
of forcibly chopping the Sikh's tresses to cause irreparable
injury to their dignity and pride. It was he every time. The
face of Dil Khush looked like his very own.

He didn't want to look at that face, therefore, he had
leaned back in his chair and stared at the tiled roof, choking
on his own grief.

*Our personal sorrows come out taking shelter of other
people's sorrows. We never get to know for which sorrow our
tears flowed. From which river the clouds filled. Into which river
they would fall.*

Dil Khush had fallen silent after some time. He did not
see a way out. Basar Mal did not have a word to offer.

He had wanted to tell Dil Khush, but could not, that
he too was receiving threatening phone calls for ten years
now—that previously it was an occasional call in six months
or a year, now it is every five or six days—that they could
even kill him.

Basar Mal Jetharam Purswani hears laughter again, this
time from behind the books. The same laughter that he
now so well recognized. But today, he pretends not to have
heard it. He does not want to hear even that revenant sweet
laughter.

He is in memory's shelter, not glorious but defeated.
What was lived was not a victory. What was not lived, that
too was a defeat. Memory makes and unmakes with all of

them. The only sanctuary in which one builds an altered desired definition. Victory is actually a name for defeat.

He jerks his head. The shake in his legs has succumbed to gooseflesh of a shiver. The corner of his mouth twitches intermittently.

Mangan's Ma is sitting with her pipe on the street. Basar Mal goes and sits next to her, resolving in his mind that this time he will curse them, abuse them, and have them reported.

For a long time, they both remain silent, drowning in themselves. At intervals, Basal Mal prays to his Jhulelal, implores Jalo to sing, and his train of thoughts winding through wakeful exhaustion, starting—stopping—starting again, keeps spooling out of nowhere:

Wakefulness runs a narrow bridge tying two sleeps.
I tread on it, a weary old man, supported on a stick.
The day yawns and the bridge wobbles.
The clacking stick keeps the pace
on legs. The shaky bridge resonates
footsteps walking on.

My days arrive like pebbles, indistinct and shapeless.
I look at them from a distance, sometimes
retreating so far that I mistake a heavy rocky day
for a loose pebble.

The injury borne of a beguiling rock
doesn't look like a pebble wound
no matter how far I withdraw.

Hot with deceit, foreheads
that furl on my name,
swathe them cool, dear Jhulelal!

The distant day grows fainter. Is past.
The sun was present in that past. Heat was
an event of that past.
The present is a humid dark left by the past heat.
All night, the dark and I, kneeling
next to each other, curse the damp matches.

Someone asked me, are you guilty
that you cannot sleep?
The guilty will be fortunate
if they received wakeful nights.
Those who are not innocent also fall asleep.

Whenever I hold your face in my palms
I feel I am offering all my memories
to the fire of our love.
You kissed my tears to start the holy fire.
You laughed
and became a land of rippling waters.

I don't know if tears have salt in them
but they have glue. She would rest my
every tear on the warm tip of her tongue
and stick it in the sky as a star.

The stars blink
because they can't meet me in the eye.
I know the story of every glistening star.

The dazzle disturbs my vision.

The soul forever a stranger in this body
as I in crowded mazes of my city.

Sing a little louder, dear sweet-voiced one,
the crickets are nibbling away my nights.

Black arcs of kohl
hold the dreams of your eyes.
The little kohl that floated out your left eye,
don't you worry about it.
From the black pit of dreams, tell me
has anyone emerged unstained?

* * *

Basar Mal's thoughts scud through a nameless night.

Mangan's Ma sits the same way on her haunches at the edge of the street. She has turned off the plastic tap of the pipe.

Perhaps she is tired of the street.

23

MY NAME IS 'I'

'Most of us knew only the river and the damaged roads and what lay beside them. Beyond that was the unknown, it could surprise us.'

—V.S. Naipaul, *A Bend in the River*

I dodge out of the house, escaping my Pau. He has been running off at the mouth again.

Today, the compound of the library is absolutely clean. Cleared of the sand and gravel and cobbles. Inside, the room is bare of cement bags. The ballasts have gone to the building across.

But there is no building across. No wall. Not even the window. There is bamboo scaffolding, the poles, looking like bars, tied to one another. Everything behind it can be distinctly seen. Even the bedroom where I had sat the other day. But it is stark. No bed, no computer, and no picture adorning the wall. The floor is strewn with caked sand, cement, and pieces of broken brick—like the Mumbai street dry after a rain, blotchy with many hues.

For a moment I see her, just standing so, at the window, the same half-open eyes as if waiting for a deep sleep after centuries of restless wakefulness, and I tell her:

When your feet are tired after standing for centuries
I will come as the grounded comfort of sitting down

She disappears. For a couple more moments, I stare at the scene and then enter the library.

The old man is sleeping in his chair. His arms make a pillow on the table, and his head is bowed down on them. I can see cement dust in places from where the bags had been hefted. The dust has ridged in the shape of the bags.

And that stubborn dust pervades the room.

I thought the noise of my arrival would wake the old man. But it looks like he's in a really deep sleep. I sit down facing him, riffle through the paper, and then drift to the window. There is no activity across. Dusk has already fallen. The masons and the workers are gone for the day.

The old man has still not stirred. Has he died? There is no telling. I shake him vigourously by the shoulders. He awakens with a start and sits up straight. 'What is the matter, Uncle? Catching up on sleep?'

He is still ruffled. His forehead bathes in sweat, as if he is frightened to see me, as if he has woken from a frightening dream.

He wipes his sweat with the handkerchief. Swills down water from a bottle.

There is a palpable sense of gloom all around. The absence of the cement bags has, as though, filled the room with grey emptiness.

'Looks like the folks have begun their renovation work,' I say to him.

He stares out the window from his chair but does not respond. He gets up, brushes the dust from his clothes, and dodders to the window, clacking his stick. He fidgets at the window for some time before retiring to his chair again. And then he sits quietly, playing with his magnifying glass.

'Are you feeling alright?'

He smiles absently.

His face is a dull grey of gloom. Like the dust that came out of the cement bags. 'Any news of Dil Khush, Uncle?' I ask.

His head bobbles from side-to-side in a no.

He plays with paper, with pencil and eraser, with the cup-shaped thermos lid, and with the few strands on his head. At length, he says—

'The window will no longer reside in the wall.'

'Hmm. Perhaps they are building a big balcony.'

'Hmm.'

He lapses into silence again. Fussing with his things for some more time, he says,

'That window was the most beautiful thing in this city.'

I look at his face. On that face, I can see the rubble of the broken wall and window. And the cloud of dust blowing from it. The hammer had fallen not on the wall but his face. When the first brick had come loose from the wall, a drop of blood would have run down his face.

He gropes for words. As though he's lost all his words in the heavy rifeness of dust. As though he's struggling to recall them.

. . . But that girl will now look out from a bigger window, Uncle!

I am tempted to say, but at the moment cannot.

24

DIL KHUSH

'It was that clear voice, so beautiful that it was almost sad. Shimamura waited for an echo to come back.'

—Yasunari Kawabata, *Snow Country*

Dil Khush's whereabouts remain unknown. He has gone missing for many days now. The advertisement of his disappearance has come in the newspapers and gone. The public excitement has died down, and so have the various conjectures which were making rounds. Whether he lives or dies doesn't matter to the state. In its records, he is gone. And people have forgotten him completely.

Today, after several days, I have come to this side of town and find that Dil Khush's shop no longer exists. Instead, an extravagant glasshouse-like eatery stands. It is called Wow, aptly so, for anyone's mouth would reflexively open in admiration looking at its beauty. I can see a good crowd inside. A bunch of twentysomethings are going about their tasks efficiently. A girl in a red blazer sits at the counter, briskly dispensing with the orders to customers queued on the other side through a small window. Some chairs have been placed for people who like to sit down and eat. The place gleams bright—clean white marble, smart red uniforms. But I can't see any kitchen. I can't spot any six-foot tall kettle. I can't hear any clanging.

I go to the counter. All kinds of fast food are available, though Wow is known primarily for its vada pav and espresso tea. The Group's eateries and shopping malls already spot the suburban Mumbai. I had read in the newspaper about its plans to recast the local ethnic vada pav as an international fast food. The wall over the counter is ornamented with laminated newspaper cuttings and illuminated with accent lighting. One says—'Wow: A desi answer to McD and KFC . . .' Another screams—'Red revolution hits Mumbai suburbs . . .' captioning a team photo of the 'men in red' making V signs. Next to it is a writeup in a regional newspaper (with the headline 'Local Vada pav Goes Global') about Wow being nation's first eating joint to export its vada pav.

The sight somehow evokes memories of the pictures that hung in Dil Khush's shop.

Close attention is given to neatness here. Dil Khush's vada pav was plonked sometimes on a plate, sometimes on a piece of paper, and sometimes straight in the hand; now there is a proper system, smooth and clinical, and the vada pav is wrapped neatly in a paper napkin and stuck with a toothpick.

The menu has been revamped as well. It boasts a new item called Samburger: a fusion of samosa with burger. Then there are puffs and many variations of pizza and burger, and some Chinese and South Indian items too.

I buy a paper napkin-wrapped, toothpick-stuck vada pav and come out of the eatery. The vada pav is costlier now by three rupees, yet it sells better. I amble to the library munching my vada pav and notice the balcony of the opposite house is complete. That house now looks more beautiful than before. For a long time, I stand there but my eye picks up no movement in its curtains.

I go in, to the old man. He is sitting as always—as one says of a stopped clock. I let him know that I'd been to the new eatery. He doesn't say anything. He is lost in his drawing book, sketching something in pencil, then erasing it. I sneak a glance at it; he is trying to make a turbaned Sardar.

He sees me peeping over and says apologetically, 'To date I haven't made a sketch of a Sardar.'

Something like an exceedingly worn-out smile sheds from his face.

'Are you sketching Dil Khush?'

He doesn't answer. One of his strokes goes wrong again. He erases it. Erasing, re-erasing, he whitens the whole page, then dodders slowly to the window. He's grown greyer, more stooped, treading the six steps between his chair and the window.

'Did you also see the house?'

'Yes. It's been built very well.'

The old man looks at me, greatly astonished. I had praised the new house; evidently, he did not like it. I go stand behind him. He continues to look out with unwavering eyes. Perhaps he searched for the window that once resided in that wall.

'But Uncle, maybe that girl comes to this window too?' I chaff him.

He goes back to his chair.

'I didn't look out to see her. I looked out to see the window . . . that you'll never understand. You aren't one of those who will love a piece of wall or a window shutter or a tiny bit of paper.'

Naturally, I am mighty offended by his words.

'Perhaps, I don't even need to,' I snap back, 'Loving humans is enough for me, thank you!'

But I know I'd just lied. Almost always alone, I spend my aloneness with Imbelo, that isn't a human but my imagination. I love my imaginations, but still want to negate the old man's love for the window. Why? It will be a long time before I'll know the answer.

The old man regards me with utter disbelief. 'When people we love cease to be, we try to seek them in objects. That's the reason we fall in love with objects the same as with people. But let me tell you, my boy—' he bristles, 'That bedroom no longer faces this side and—and there's no window now in that girl's bedroom.'

'He He He'

I crow my proud, smug laughter.

'So what, Uncle? If not her, then someone else. Is there any dearth?'

The old man's eyes have an expression not outraged or astonished now, but like everything emptying out. He keeps staring at me.

Agreed, I had the temerity to utter a flip 'so what?' but if truth be told, an abyss has formed inside my heart. As if by a sudden, violent implosion. And the realization is fast sinking in, that the girl would not be seen at the window.

I came here only for her, and she had captured an immeasurable space in my dreams and imagination. To get courage and even hope just by looking at someone—that intense emotion I experienced only while looking at her.

However hard I may try quashing my emotions, the truth is I badly want to cry.

Why am I like this? Perhaps I don't want anyone to know my softness, so I fake a hard exterior. People's sensibilities rebounding off my hardness get wounded. My Pau's. Old Basar Mal Uncle's. They think I am cruel, careless, disrespectful, selfish. Is it really so?

It's a three-way struggle between memory, imagination, and reality.

Old Basar Mal's love is in his memory.

My love is in my imagination.

Love for us has no external reality. Essentially we both are alike, but we don't know it or don't believe it and perhaps don't also want to understand it.

A sentence such as 'We are not different from each other after all' is difficult to understand.

'Haven't you tasted Wow's vada pav yet?' I ask him, to change the conversation. The woebegoneness of my voice does not change.

He shakes his head and reverts to his drawing book. He is again having a go at drawing his Sardar.

'He is a very young and dynamic entrepreneur, this Wow fellow. And that's one badass idea. Making even vada pav global. Great! This is what we call a business strategy, no Uncle?'

But he remains silent. Entangled in his sketch. I stand behind him; his hand pauses. He does not raise his head but remains like that—paused—and lets out an audible sigh. I remove myself from there and resituate across, facing him. His hand again starts moving. This time swiftly, purposefully. As if he has found the line that will let him reenter the sketch. Now, he is not looking up at all.

And, I am not looking at him either. That yellow window, its large-flowered lattice, the yellow fluttering curtains and the yellow face pan before my eyes, again and again. It feels someone is very slowly removing my skin.

25

MY NAME IS 'I'

'With all my baggage gone I can travel light now, forging on deeper into the forest. I focus on moving forward. No need to mark any more trees, no need to remember the path back. I don't even look at my surroundings.'

—Haruki Murakami, *Kafka on the Shore*

At last, I defeated my Pau.

It is such a relief.

After spending eight months in Kolkata, where I hold an excellent job, I have briefly returned home. I feel elated with my six-lakh-rupee pay deal: there is a kind of pride in it. I don't know how many times I've told Pau that in the contemporary scene, the world sought the potency and the dynamic impatience of young people. But he wouldn't believe me—my Pau always saw the world through his foggy old glasses.

At work, I lead a small team of twelve, all veterans twice my age or nearly my Pau's. I am a neophyte, but still, I'm their boss. Grasping a file, when those dab hands stand to attention before me, reverent and silent, a smile automatically plays on my face. My apotheosis has adopted a patronizing kindness towards them. So, I speak to them with an added dollop of affection and, prevailing over their diffidence, offer them my favourite Jasmine-flavoured green tea, which I prepare myself. They look joyous, overwhelmed, even grateful.

:-)

Bashful and watery-eyed, they stand, slightly hunching their shoulders, and when they sit, they keep their backs straight without leaning in the chair. They are never the first to shake hands, but greet bowing their heads slightly, and never enter my cabin without asking permission. I tell them to call me by my first name, but they always address me as sir, and among themselves, often refer to me as their big boss even though I am a junior in the lower rungs of the company. In meetings, they display an eagerness to take down notes, and only after I laugh do they titter. Timidly, respectfully, they proffer advice, whereas my job is to accept their counsel, taking advantage of their experience, and then, hand the same back to them as an order. They readily forget that it was their own counsel, rather believe it was a product of my fertile and sharp mind and thus never lay claim to their ideas and thoughts—at least, they act that way!

When they look at me, with their eyes filled with hope, it seems they are looking at their own son.

When I look at them, I feel I am looking at my Pau.

I narrate to Pau stories of my ascension, and he listens to them attentively, his eyes shining with admiration all through, the way my office people watch my presentations with shining eyes. Pau reminds me so much of my subordinates, sitting the same way, stiff and upright, as though he is sitting not in his house but my office cabin.

When my Pau hugs me tight, profoundly overwhelmed, and as his awe and pride pass through his hands into me, I remember his repudiations and say, 'Frankly speaking, Pau, this hugging thing is the latest trend. A famous entrepreneur, I'm forgetting his name, was the first to establish the practice of hugging his employees; since then, almost all management gurus—from the New Age Mehras and Chopras to our Bollywood Munnabhai—have considered it better than the customary handshake for developing inter-personal relationships. Even one of the best business magazines has given it their seal of approval.'

:-)

Well pleased with myself, I gush with laughter and once again hug my Pau. But somewhere, it feels, Pau's grip on my back is a little slack this time. His hands skid limply down my proud bearing as if he is breaking himself free from my hold. He mumbles—'This is a father's love, not some inter-personal relationship.'

He sits down. I take out a cigarette from my pocket and put it to my lips, but meeting his eye, embarrassed, I keep it back. He pretends not to see anything and remains silent. I relate many more tales, and he listens, smiling softly. Behind the glasses, I can see the same shine in his eyes.

I feel my self-assurance rising once again as I tell him how by just greeting my people by their first names, or asking them about their family, they are so filled with joy and utter gratitude that they begin to consider me a benevolent father figure, to which Pau is thoughtful at first, then concedes that yes, he never paid attention to this aspect or even cared, and it's such a simple way to get one's work done!

Do I catch a hint of derision in his response, or is it the first step towards admitting defeat? I feel I can ask him openly. I am earning now, in fact, much more than him. An Indian father respects a son who earns more than him. But does he?

So I ask bluntly, 'Tell the truth, Pau, do you admit defeat?'

'What defeat, boy?' He is genuinely taken aback.

'The battle we started, Pau, you win unless I win it. And since I have succeeded in my design, you have lost the battle,' I lay it out in detail.

'Lost it? Battle we started . . . Why are you saying this, boy?' He looks innocent.

I feel bad. He has always been torturing me with his lectures and taunts, and now, at this moment, he is feigning ignorance! Anyway, I started it, and I want to finish it.

'Pau,' I begin, 'As a young boy, I had a dream one night—that we both were passing through a jungle and a lion attacked you. I jumped in between and killed it. You were wounded. I carried you on my back to the hospital. You hugged me tight, and I said to you, "You're my king. You won't get hurt as long as I'm around." And you said with pride, "Well done, my prince!"'

He listens intently. Not meeting his eye, I continue,

'The dream was only this, Pau. It was my favourite dream. But dreams are whimsical. The same dream refuses to turn up in our sleep even when we coax it. So I began to imagine that dream. There would be a new story each time, a new enemy, but the narrative remained the same. Through the years, even though the lion changed to an elephant, the elephant to a dacoit, and so on, I saved you, and you admired me for that.'

Although I had climbed down from his kingdom of shoulders, he'd been my king for a long time, and I, his prince.

'We bonded with a secret pride. I imagined this story so many times all through my life it became a part of my being.'

And then I see his face. His lips are trembling. I think for a moment that I should shut up; I don't have any right to hurt my father. But I ignore his tremble,

'Yes, I can never see myself separate from the part of a powerful prince, and even now, you look nothing more than a helpless man.'

'In my stories, I've saved your life, and you should feel grateful, Pau!' I joke weakly and try to laugh. But the atmosphere is grim and humourless. I cannot bring a smile to my lips. His lips hide their tremble. His whole manner is once again deadpan, and he waits for the story to finish.

After a moment's silence, I say,

'I don't know when fighting for you turned into fighting against you. I don't know when stand-by-your-side changed positions and became stand-facing-you. I haven't understood, Pau, why you want to defeat me? Prove me wrong every time? Show me useless? Scorn my decisions? Dismiss my efforts? Now, see, in your desire to defeat me, you yourself are defeated! See for yourself.'

I speak to him the way I speak to my people in the office and wait for a long reproach, a lecture or a fresh taunt, for being a dimwit and dreamy and pointless.

But nothing like that happens. We sit facing each other. There is nothing in between us. Surprisingly, I find no wall, no window, no door, no cave that has to be opened by uttering some magic words. Really, there is nothing.

Pau looks pale. There is something in his haggard manner that speaks of a hurt, an exhaustion. He rises to his feet, pats me on the shoulder, and shuffles towards the door. Abruptly he turns around and says—'Quit smoking, boy, or do a good quality.'

Can he ever resist admonishing me?

'I'm doing Benson and Hedges, Pau. *The Best!*' I return, grinning broadly.

:-)

But he does not smile back. He bows his head, then, turning around once again, trudges towards the door. At the door, he pauses, gazes at me for a while, and says,

'When you were young, I saw a dream. Perhaps we both saw the same dream on the same night at the same time. The only difference was in my dream, you were attacked by the lion, and it was I who saved you.'

I am thunderstruck by his words. Unconsciously, I take out the cigarette from my pocket. Pau does not say anything and, bowing his head, goes out the door. He seems older, more helpless while retreating. Like that old man of the library. The glimpse I catch of his face is pale, almost yellow, like that face at the yellow window.

For a long time I remain seated, uncomprehending and spent. Perhaps it is I who sit in the chair helpless like the old man? Is it my face which is yellow, secretly borrowing the colour from the girl?

Can we really defeat anyone? Damn.

Am I a smarty-pants? Or plain stupid? Or both?

Who am I to say who's right and who's wrong?

Although one day, I will know it. I am sure I will know (because one should know when there's time) that the struggle in our lives is, often, a struggle between right and right. That it is not between good and bad, but many times between two goods.

I light the cigarette and storm out of the house.

On an impulse, I catch a taxi for the first time from Flora Fountain to Nariman Point. Earlier, I relished this stretch by foot. It seems like a long time ago. Perhaps I have lost the habit of walking. Or changed that habit.

The sidewalks, which used to be vibrant against the columned backdrop of books, look biggish and sombre. I heard the bookstalls were ruthlessly cleared away. What else is lost? I wonder. I look for the page where my life changed: a change I am not yet consciously aware of.

The evening breeze is a relief.

At Nariman Point, the waves of the Arabian Sea rise and die with a voracity. I walk towards the sea, my back heavy with exhaustion. Bags of exhaustion hang from my elbows, waist and calves. The sea is a friend, a comforter. No one can hear our wailing except the sea. The sea's clamour is a clump of our orphaned cries. I look out on the sea seeking to recognize—amidst the sweeping sounds—strands of my own faint cry. I think of the people I left just like that, people who left me, and I think of the changes happening inside. I do not know if my voice will reach those whom I love, but by the time the sun goes down like a wreathe of fire, I am lost in the prolonged drone of the sea that sucks me into unreal surroundings, my life lying so, hoisted on the cries of waves, the imaginary cave swinging in and out of the line of sight—was it there before? Not now? Is it there now? Not before?

I watch my revamped world through a watery membrane trembling between the sight and the scene. About me, the neon lights shimmer in a wide crescent of the Queen's Necklace, and the teashops are being lit up with lanterns—

There is so much shine that I want to pull apart the fibres of light to see which part of it is black.

26

THE BOOK COVER TELLS A TALE

'The struggle of man against power is the struggle of memory against forgetting.'
—Milan Kundera, *The book of Laughter and Forgetting*

Something happened yesterday that reminds me of a very old story. Let me recount it for you:

Long ago, there was a girl called Neel Sar. Neel Sar in Sanskrit means 'The blue lake'. Ravishing, pristine, bright as the sun, the fame of her beauty was far and wide. Nobody had seen her, and nobody knew if she was real or just a fable. Only her servant knew, an extremely trustworthy and faithful man, and he had done well to keep her secret.

She often danced in her huge mansion and one day, relenting to her servant's supplications, she allowed him to watch her through a secret hole in the wall of her room.

That fluid–like dance had an ethereal brilliance; it was as if his servile life's divine sensation, and from then on, he lived night and day intoxicated with memories of that dance.

One day, he unwittingly blurted out this secret to the king, the raja of the land, that his mistress was not a fiction but a living woman. A singular beauty and a superlative dancer. Now, the king was insistent that he should see her dance. And despite his reluctance, the servant had to accede to this untenable demand to save his life. The king, you see, was a despot.

And so, the king watched Neel Sar through the same hole. Neel Sar could sense someone watching her, and she at once stopped her dance. But the king was already besotted with her. Now he was insistent that she should marry him, that she should give him her fine mansion—a mansion that, despite sporting a homely exterior, had such expansive, magnificently sweeping interiors that even the kingdom of Indra, the king of heaven, looked tiny in comparison. But Neel Sar vehemently refused. Whereupon the king, becoming furious, forcibly tried to obtain her. The faithful servant intervened, and he was killed. Neel Sar, for her active resistance, was torched.

If something fancied cannot be gained, a king will destroy it. The power, and might intoxicate many into thinking they are kings. Mothers overindulge their sons, call them 'my prince', 'my raja beta', and raise them as such. By doing so, they unknowingly fill them with a tyrant's traits and iniquities—ergo, such children, on growing up, harbour a desire to destroy what they cannot obtain. Have you noticed a child will catch a butterfly by the wings, then set it free? As an adult, he will catch people, and rip out their wings.

You might ask, how does the foregoing story have any relation with mine? There is always an unseeable thread between any two stories that mysteriously binds one to the other. When that thread becomes visible to the eye, the bond is then easily understood, which, at times, is a curiously remarkable one. As between this story and mine.

In the diachronic events that occurred after Neel Sar perished, she was born again centuries later. As a book. The world's first book or second or third or fourth, heaven knows which one, but she became a book. The king is reborn, always, as a king. As far as I know.

Neel Sar had been so traumatized by that destructive incident in her life that she had vowed never to be born in the human form again. So now Neel Sar, reborn a book, lived in the Assyrian capital, Nineveh, in the library of Ashurbanipal. Like her, many books lived there in the form of clay tablets, copperplates, and birch-barks. When in a series of attacks the neighbouring states destroyed the empire, they also burned down the library. Neel Sar, in her next birth, was again a book and went to live in the library of Alexandria. But she was burned again. And again. She was burned in Nalanda when a king set fire to its massive library: the flames could not be doused for one whole year. In the Buddhist monasteries in the Maldives, a troublesome king arrived; he would break a Buddha idol, along with it, behead five monks, and with it, burn 500 books. There were hundreds of idols, thousands of monks, and millions of books. Believe me, they were all Neel Sar.

When Mongols reached Baghdad, they burned all its libraries and threw the books in the Tigris. Its waters remained black for six months from the ink that kept streaking out of the pages and mixing into the water. Yes, they were Neel Sar's chopped hair. World wars happened; every country dropped bombs on the libraries of every other country. In Jaffna, a group of agitators went in police uniforms and torched a whole library. A few years ago, in Egypt, to oppose military rule, the so-called supporters of democracy lit the largest library housed in the heart of Cairo. These people, who raised slogans of humanity and compassion, then danced around the book bonfire, and the whole world watched their dance 'live' on their television sets. Then again, another terrorist group was marshalled to torch books in Mosul.

Soon, no part of the world remained where blood wasn't shed. No part of the world remained where books didn't burn. Sometimes, the mullah of a mosque burned them. Sometimes, the padre of a church. Or sometimes, the mahant of a temple. The soldiers burned them. The politicians burned them. The wealthy and the slaves burned them. And the workers. And the Nazis. Protesting against them, the communists. Against them, the democrats. Supporting terror, the terrorists. Opposing terror, the self-styled patriots. A Neel Sar lives inside every burned book. That king lives inside every person who burned it. They bespeak the filiation of this historical tale through time.

The game goes on in every birth, birth after birth. Neel Sar and I are one. I can go on recounting as many tales of Neel Sar (or mine) as the drops in the Great Ocean. Would it make any difference to anyone?

I would in every life face fire's fierce obliteration and once again experience the resplendence of creation. Every time, my words would be wombed and born again, stronger by fire and prouder in resistance.

But why am I telling you all this? Because yesterday, I saw the shadow of fire.

Basar Mal had sat at his table as usual, with eyes downcast, taking off his glasses and stowing them neatly on the book he'd been reading. We books, like inanimate statues, had lain motionless in our places. The boy no longer came to the library. Our solitude seemed unfazed by the shadows—far from the polity of sights and sounds. In this hushed stagnancy, a fat fellow tramped in unannounced and installed himself in front of Basar Mal. He had the imperious bearing of a king. Finding this unexpected visitor before him, Basar Mal's eyes betrayed shadows of a latent fear that had been hounding him secretly. But the fat man didn't say anything. He simply sat toying with Basar Mal's glasses. The old man sat silently.

No storm howled along. No scary background music played. That man didn't wear any dramatic expression. Basar Mal had by then smoothened his own emotions. A page fluttered in a corner wanting to tear free from its binding. The coffee left in the cup was drying. Hanging limply to one side on the window, the fabric, used rarely as a curtain, sighed at its hem. The great writers looked down from their photo frames at the scene. A dry leaf flew, sometimes this side, sometimes that side on the floor. A fly was buzzing near the door. The cars whizzed by on the street. Local trains rolled on at their pace viciously. In some part of the city, a girl was escaping from lecherous lads. A man was eating food out of his lunchbox. A lost child was stammering his parents' address to the police, and nobody understood. Another child was playing with a football that came as a gift. Fishermen were casting their nets in the Arabian sea. The fish themselves were swimming towards the trap.

The business of the world was as usual. The usual was ostensibly tranquil.

An unmistakable shadow of a little flame heaved in the room of this library. No one could sense it, save me. You see, with fire, I have old ties. And I can recognize its flames by its shadow.

For long the obtrusive presence sat playing with the old man's spectacles. And the old man silently watched his presumptuous play. All of a sudden, that fat fellow rose and touched the old man's feet. He wanted to be blessed. While bowing, he murmured something in reverential tones. While straightening, his eyes sweeping us had shadows of a conflagration.

The silent man, arriving as the everyday bustle, had bent down like a humble threat. My experienced mind was conscious of a rushing fire: fire that turned Neel Sar's body in her every birth into ash. The spies of fire are always aware of her whereabouts.

I am Neel Sar.

I am Basar Mal's scented consciousness.

I am the boy's caress.

I am the girl standing at the yellow window.

I am many things—All the things—Yet do not know what I am.

I wish to speak to the boy one last time. I doubt if this is possible anymore. I doubt if the boy will ever come here. The yellow window does not live in the wall opposite. And the window from Larkana will not travel here.

The girl framed at the window is forever destroyed.

That outline had been of a desire, not the desired: a beguiling illusion he was drawn to, which he had drawn himself. It was like imagining a story based on a portrait— the analytical picture game that we play as children—a charming image not enough to be reduced to merely one story but many different ones as his imagination pleased.

I wish to meet the boy like a book, like a human, like the girl standing at the yellow window, and tell him just this much—

If ever you remember me,
touch a favourite book
and begin reading it.
A word of love
in any language
will eventually
always bring you to me.

I am born of a tree, I'll become ash and meld with earth.

Basar Mal is born out of earth; he will sink back into earth. I feel saddened to see that his soul will always remain a refugee.

That boy is made from desires; he'll be oscillating in an almost endless monotonous existence. With the wisdom of hindsight, he will know that the end is always an illusion.

The girl framed by the window is made out of someone's imagination. Stuck between earth and sky like a kite without a string, she'll see herself disintegrate slowly—

As I see myself incinerating now.

Air sweeps away everything.

The ocean swallows everything.

One day, earth would shroud everything.

27

MY NAME IS 'I'

'Whether the citizen lives or dies is not a concern of the state. What matters to the state and its records is whether the citizen is alive or dead.'

—J.M. Coetzee, *Diary of a Bad Year*

After that I never went there again.

I do not know what happened to the girl. I had loved her intensely for those many days, but I never went there. I loved—as long as I loved—drowning myself in love. I cannot say I loved drowning myself in a street or river. I cannot also say if my love was a reality or an imagination.

When she said every street walked from its place to tie in a bun at her nape, I wasn't with her. When I ran my hand in her hair, and the street-like hair stuck in my fingers, I wasn't with her even then. When she said 'and . . .' expectantly, I wasn't there to requite that 'and . . .'

I was, in truth, nowhere.

I was forever in my corporate pleasure, in an endless nebulous gratification.

Was Basar Mal there or not? I do not know. But I wasn't with Basar Mal.

The day the JCB machine reached Sindhu Library, I wasn't there.

The ballast was heaped up in front of the machine. A million gunny bags of cement were unloaded and dumped. From the gunny bags, the dust of cement had blown. Some settled on books, some stuck to adjacent buildings.

A portentous labour was under way.

The books were pulled out from inside and rounded up in the compound. They were doused in kerosene and set on fire.

The iron closets were weighed and given to the scrap merchants; the wooden table and the chairs were incinerated along with the books.

Whether the old walls of the library crumbled with a mere touch of the machine, or whether they stood upright for long, challenging the cold strength of the alloy, no one knows.

And whatever happened to the board that announced the name of the library in three languages?

How did the books dance their last dance of mourning? On which rhythm of neglect and beats of despair was their swansong? Did they, like those angels, manage to smother their feelings and pretend a celebration?

In a matter of hours, the library that had been running for years was reduced to rubble—ash, brick, gravel, stone, broken tiles. Now there was the thick reek of burnt paper. There was the odour of pervading dust.

The street changed.

The Wow group was constructing an ultra-modern shopping mall where the library had once stood. A young business house under a dynamic leadership. Their shopping malls now mushroomed across the city at a fierce speed—a five-storey structure, where condom to car was to be touted, whose first storey was for a state-of-the-art parking lot, and whose terrace was to accommodate a trendy round-the-clock discotheque.

A forty-foot-deep pit was dug out for the foundation. But no one knows what filled up this pit.

Because there was no one present at the time. There was no such library. No such event that happened. No such record.

The writings have since turned to dust. Sepulchered in it are the silent souls and the fallen stars—fallen because their dreams have broken.

Those in love with a piece of wall, a window shutter, or bits of paper will understand when I say these walls and windows and papers also have souls. Do they flit among the rubble here late at night? Why does the watchman guarding the construction site suddenly wake up, alarmed, in the middle of the night and stand there nervously, blowing his whistle?

Was also the fragrance of guava, of coffee, of tobacco buried in there? Or do these fragrances still wander in the hot, dusty air whimpering, desirous to be sniffed just once fervently?

I do not know the answers to these questions. Nobody does. Because there was no one there at that time. Neither Basar Mal nor I.

Basar Mal was gone long before this. No one knows where. Just as, before him, Dil Khush was gone one day and no one ever found him again.

TRANSLATOR'S NOTE

This is the first presentation in English of a full-length fiction by Geet Chaturvedi, who is a major writer in Hindi today. A slim volume, its evolution is interesting. The book has its genesis in the long poem *Sindhu Library* that Geet wrote in 1998. It was converted into a long-short story in 2007 and published in *Pragatisheel Vasudha* a year later. In 2010, it was presented as a novella in his collection *Pink Slip Daddy*. In 2016, the English translation won a PEN/Heim Translation Fund Grant awarded by PEN America.

As ideas and images once again slowly found their way into the Hindi text, the initial 20,000-word story called *Simsim* grew almost three times in size and became a novel. This translation follows the standalone novel of 2022. The additions, however, happened almost simultaneously in both the original and the translation, and they have had delightful effects on the story. Because of the dynamicity, the translated text may not match line for line with the original, but those discrepancies would be minor.

But is the story complete now? Who is to say? Each time the story pauses, it is given a beautiful turn and left. *Art exists in this incompleteness.* The translation here journeys all the way to the current turn.

The story takes place in Mumbai and in Larkana, and Geet uses Sindhi, Urdu, and Mumbaiya abundantly to differentiate the varied linguistic backgrounds of the characters. A splash of these dialects allows his linguistic reality to be in touch with its grassroots. I have had the usual difficulties with the language spoken by the refugees, rioters, the chai-samosa wallahs, and the working middle class. My approach has been to use the simple Indian English, as spoken by the masses in India, sometimes giving the slangy expressions and idioms a literal translation. At the same time, I have aimed not to cast the dialogues into an English that feels wrong.

Some English phrases used in the original have been retained as such. For example, the typical Indian English phrase 'solid dialogue' may not sound natural in perfect English but fits here, I must say, quite well. Swear words are the easiest to translate; they almost always find an equivalent in English. The vocabulary of the offence is rich in any language.

At the level of language, the text of *Simsim* shifts effortlessly from distinguished, literary Hindi to colloquial speech. Then there are inflections from sharp, rhythmic sentences, rendering the text almost poetic. Geet is a poet at heart. The few poems set in *Simsim* are lines sitting mysteriously in the surrounding prose, sometimes prophesying, sometimes drumming an abstract silence.

Above all, there are frequent shifts in the pace of the narrative. On the one hand, we have the delicate textuality in the characterizations that take shape in a kind of leisureliness, be it Mangan's Ma tending to her plastic doll or Basar Mal sitting among his tattered books; on the other, there is the fiercely eventful riot flashback or the emotional drama between 'I' and his Pau. I have translated these pauses and changes of speed whenever I could; I find that the engagement with changing topography of the text and the associated translative practices extend the experience.

I want to mention three things. First, the Hindi *Simsim* embeds a quotation from another text at the beginning of each chapter and is reproduced in English translation. *Simsim* is an elegy for books. Second, the novel's title comes from the story 'Ali Baba and the Forty Thieves' in the *Arabian Nights*. The command 'Open Sesame' (English), *'Khul Ja Simsim'* (Hindi), or *'Iftah Ya Simsim'* (Arabic) was used to call out to the magical door of the cave to open. Third, the thoughts on completeness and incompleteness appearing in the book have their roots in the Upanishads. Incompleteness is also a theme in Deleuze and Guattari's philosophy, which, in turn, was influenced by Riemann's mathematics.

* * *

There is a phrase in Sanskrit: '*Parkaya Pravesh*', which means letting your soul enter another body. As a translator, I feel this is a two-way process—first, to let the soul of the text merge with my soul, so to speak, and then let that merged soul go back into the body of the text, but in my language.

I enjoy this reversal. An endeavour known as translation has its enchantments.

Anita Gopalan
30 July 2022

LIST OF QUOTATIONS

Chapter 1: Ben Okri, *The Famished Road*, (London: Vintage, 2003), p. 3.

Chapter 2: Primo Levi, *The Drowned and the Saved*, Translated from the Italian by Michael F. Moore, *The Complete Works of Primo Levi*, (New York: Liveright Publishing Corporation, W.W. Norton and Company, 2015), p. 2568.

*Nirmal Verma. The quote in the chapter is translated by Anita Gopalan from the Hindi book *Itihas, Smriti, Akanksha*, (New Delhi: National Publishing House, 1996), p. 24.

Chapter 3: Imre Kertész, *Liquidation*, translated from the Hungarian by Tim Wilkinson, (London: Harvill Secker, 2006), p. 27.

Chapter 4: Marcel Proust, *Swann's Way*, translated from the French by Lydia Davis, (London: Penguin Books, 2004), p. 407.

Chapter 5: Imre Kertész, *Liquidation*, translated from the Hungarian by Tim Wilkinson, (London: Harvill Secker, 2006), p. 19.

Chapter 6: Elif Shafak, *The Bastard of Istanbul*, (London: Penguin Viking, 2007), p. 1.

Chapter 7: Günter Grass, *Peeling the Onion*, translated from the German by Michael Henry Heim, (London: Vintage, 2008), p. 3.

Chapter 8: Peter Handke, 'Song of Childhood', A recurring poem in Wings of Desire (Der Himmel über Berlin), a film directed by Wim Wenders. Originally written in German, the English words are from the subtitles.

Chapter 10: Pär Lagerkvist, *The Death of Ahasuerus*, translated from the Swedish by Naomi Walford, (New York: Vintage Books, 1982) p. 12.

Chapter 11: Amos Oz, *A Tale of Love and Darkness*, translated from the Hebrew by Nicolas de Lange, (London: Vintage, 2005), p. 22.

Chapter 12: Nirmal Verma. The quoted line is translated by Anita Gopalan from the Hindi book *Dhundh Se Uthti Dhun* (Lit: A Tune Arising from the Mist), (New Delhi: Rajkamal Prakashan, 1997), p. 18.

Chapter 13: Umberto Eco, *The Name of the Rose*, translated from the Italian by William Weaver, Page 438, Vintage, London, 1998.

Chapter 14: Jean Genet, *The Thief's Journal*, Translated from the French by Bernard Frechtman, Page 7, Grove Press, New York, 1994.

Chapter 15: Naomi Klein, *No Logo*, Page 49, Picador, New York, 2002.

Chapter 16: Italo Calvino, 'The Argentine Ant', Translated from the Italian by Archibald Colquhoun, Page 96, from the collection *The Watcher and Other Stories*, Harvest Book, New York, 1975.

Chapter 17: Carlos Fuentes, *The Years with Laura Diaz*, translated from the Spanish by Alfred Mac Adam, (New York: Farrar, Straus and Giroux, 2000), p. 6.

Chapter 18: Kahlil Gibran, *Sand and Foam*, (Melbourne: William Heinemann, 1957), p. 18.

Chapter 19: Bhau Padhye, 'Five Gardens'. The quoted line is translated by Anita Gopalan based on the Hindi translation of the Marathi original by Geet Chaturvedi from the book *Bhau Padhye Yanchya Shreshtha Katha*, Edited by Dilip Purushottam Chitre, (Mumbai: Lok Vangmaya Griha, 2004), p. 42.

Chapter 20: Samuel Beckett, *Molloy*, translated from the French by Patrick Bowels in collaboration with the author, (London: Faber and Faber, 2009), p. 194.

Chapter 21: Toni Morrison, *Beloved*, (New York: Vintage International, 2004), p. 30.

Chapter 22: U. R. Ananthamurthy, *Samskara*, the line quoted is translated by Anita Gopalan based on the Hindi translation of the Kannada original by Chandrakant

Kusnoor, (New Delhi: Radhakrishna Prakashan, 1980), p.149.

Chapter 23: V. S. Naipaul, *A Bend in the River*, (London: Picador, 2002), p. 74.

Chapter 24: Yasunari Kawabata, *Snow Country*, translated from the Japanese by Edward G. Seidensticker, (New York: Wideview/Perigee Books, 1981), p. 30.

Chapter 25: Haruki Murakami, *Kafka on the Shore*, translated from the Japanese by Philip Gabriel, (New York: Vintage International, 2005), p. 415.

The last line of the chapter is based on the following *sher* by Fazal Tabish:

Resha-Resha Udhed Kar Dekho / Roshni Kis Jagah Se Kaali Hai

Chapter 26: Milan Kundera, *The Book of Laughter and Forgetting*, translated from the Czech by Michael Henry Heim, (Middlesex, England: Penguin Books, 1981), p. 11.

Chapter 27: J. M. Coetzee, *Diary of a Bad Year*, (London: Vintage Books, 2008), p. 10.

AUTHOR'S ACKNOWLEDGEMENTS

I would like to express my gratitude to all those without whom this book could not have appeared in this form.

Dr Bhavana Pant Chaturvedi, my childhood friend and wife, who smilingly bears my madness. Swadha and Areen, my children, whose creativity inspires me.

Anita Gopalan, my friend and translator, who believed in *Simsim* more than I did, who discussed its every page— sometimes as an encouraging and affectionate friend, sometimes as a bloodthirsty critic, and sometimes as a word-counting editor.

My late mother. And my late father, Abodh, who never lived in Sindh but spoke Sindhi fluently, who had a wealth of stories from Sindh, and who taught me to love the poetry of Shah Abdul Latif.

Late comrade Suryadev Upadhyay, who would've been more than 100 years old today and who is present in every page of this book.

Late actor–journalist Ramesh Nankani, who read to me books of Sindhi literature.

Late Prof. Kamala Prasad, editor of *Pragatisheel Vasudha*, whose loving requests shaped the old *Simsim*.

Sindhi poet Vimmi Sadarangani, with whom I had many discussions on Sindh and the old *Simsim* during 2011–13, and who made some rare books easily available from across the border.

Elder brother Vineet, younger sister Anamika, Jeevan Pandey, Guru Dutt, and Sanjay Bhise, and my Marathi translator Jui Kulkarni, whose words, recollections, and attachments flow through this book, invisibly.

In the end: A 'Syed Haider Raza Fellowship' from the Raza Foundation made it possible for me to write this book. I am grateful to the Raza Foundation and Shri Ashok Vajpeyi for this prestigious fellowship.

TRANSLATOR'S ACKNOWLEDGEMENTS

I am infinitely grateful to Sanyukta Giri for her painstaking reads, proofreads, and sharp observations, and for her fine sense of words and music. Her presence in my work is immense.

I am indebted to my family, which includes my husband, two children, mother, and sixteen dogs, for providing me with joy, comfort, excitement, and laughter. I will forever cherish my late father's presence in my life and work.

And how to thank Geet Chaturvedi for his unwavering faith in me and my translations? I am grateful for our lively discussions, for his knowledge, and for his help in understanding intractable Hindi sentences.

I am thankful to PEN America for the PEN/Heim Translation Fund Grant that gave me my first recognition and helped my motivation; to *Chicago Review*, *Nashville Review*, *Sycamore Review*, and *The Offing* for publishing excerpts from the book; and above all to the art of translation that has filled my life with a new meaning.

COMMON
ACKNOWLEDGEMENTS

We would like to thank the following people: Geetanjali Shree for her love and generosity; Kanishka Gupta, Moutushi Mukherjee, Shaoni Mukherjee, Jennifer Croft, Anees Salim, Udayan Vajpeyi, and Sasha Dugdale for their kindness.

Finally—three cheers to our own '*Do Bhai Ki Dukan*'.

Sometimes during our conversations, in typical Mumbaiya style, we call each other Anita Bhai and Geet Bhai and jokingly call our literary endeavours 'Do Bhai Ki Dukan' (a shop run by two brothers), a popular name for shops found in North India, particularly in the Delhi-Haryana-Punjab belt.